Revisions—Zen for Film

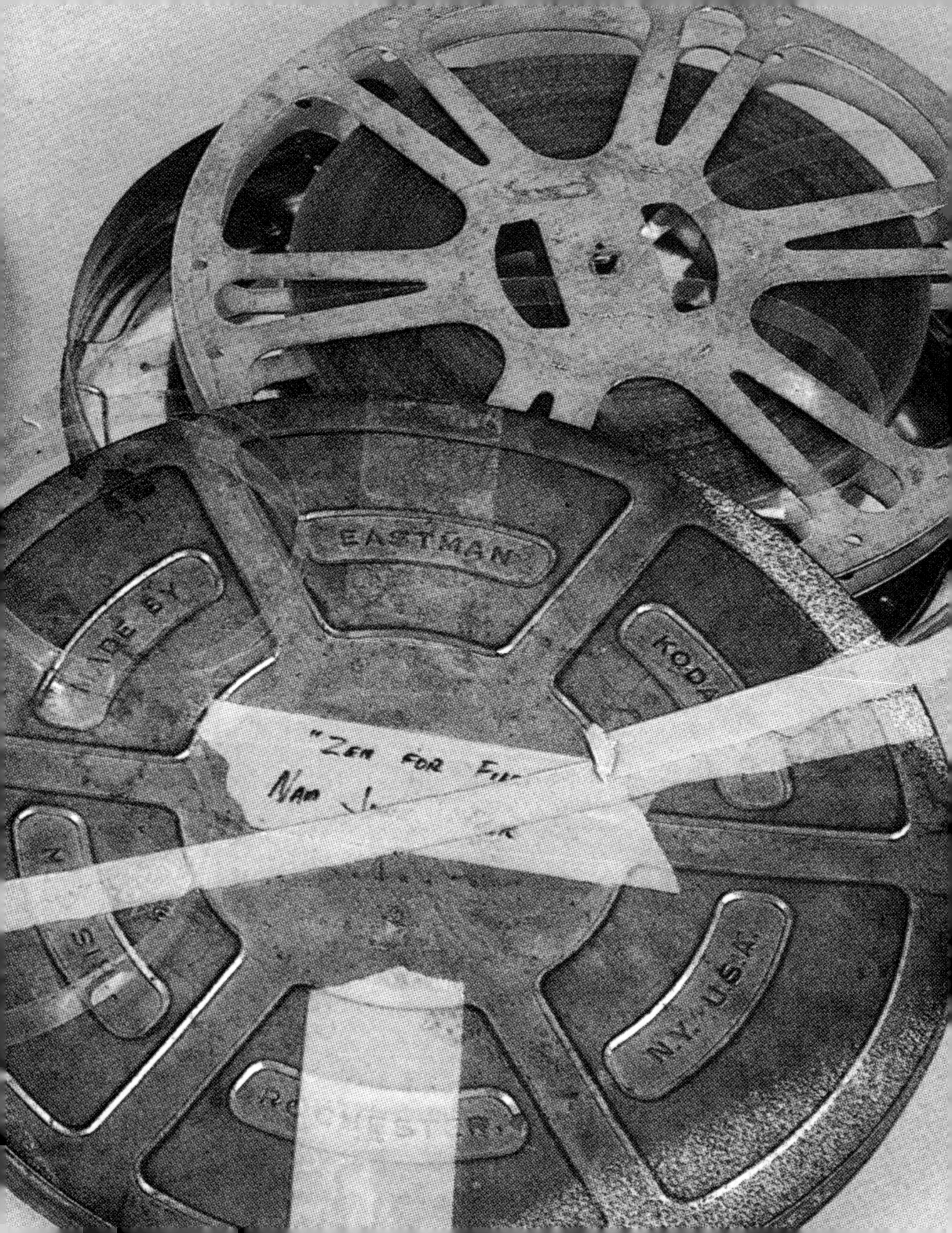
EASTMAN
N.Y. U.S.A.

Revisions—Zen for Film

Hanna B. Hölling

Published by Bard Graduate Center
New York City

This catalogue is published in conjunction with the exhibition *Revisions: Zen for Film* held at Bard Graduate Center Gallery from September 18, 2015, through January 10, 2016.

The project was developed during a two-year Andrew W. Mellon Cultures of Conservation visiting professorship at Bard Graduate Center.

Curator of the Exhibition: Hanna B. Hölling

Focus Gallery Team:
Director of the Gallery and Executive Editor, Gallery Publications: Nina Stritzler-Levine
Head of Focus Gallery Project: Ivan Gaskell
Chief Curator: Marianne Lamonaca
Focus Gallery Project Coordinator: Ann Marguerite Tartsinis (locum: Caroline Hannah)
Exhibition Designer: Ian Sullivan
Director of the Digital Media Lab: Kimon Keramidas
Dean for Academic Administration and Student Affairs: Elena Pinto Simon

Catalogue Production:
Director of Publishing: Daniel Lee
Catalogue Design and Production: Kate DeWitt and Hue Park
Manager of Rights and Reproductions: Alexis Mucha

Published by Bard Graduate Center, New York City

Typeface: This book is set in Melior, DIN Engschrift, and FF DIN.

Exclusive trade distribution by the University of Chicago Press, Chicago and London

ISBN: 978-1-941792-04-9

Library of Congress Cataloging-in-Publication Data

Hölling, Hanna.

Revisions-Zen for film / Hanna B. Hölling.

pages cm

Includes bibliographical references and index.

1. Paik, Nam June, 1932-2006. Zen for film--Exhibitions. 2. Experimental films--United States--Exhibitions. 3. Artists' materials--Deterioration--Exhibitions. I. Bard Graduate Center: Decorative Arts, Design History, Material Culture, host institution, organizer. II. Title. III. Title: Zen for film.

PN1998.3.P3452H65 2015

791.43'72--dc23

2015019717

Printed by GHP, West Haven, Connecticut

Cover Image: Peter Moore. Nam June Paik casting shadows on *Zen for Film* at the New Cinema Festival I, Film-Makers' Cinematheque, New York, November 2, 1965. © CNAC/MNAM/Dist. RMN-Grand Palais / Art Resource, NY. © Barbara Moore / Licensed by VAGA, New York, NY. © 2015 Nam June Paik Estate.

Title Spread Image: Nam June Paik. *Zen for Film*, 1964. Photograph by Brad Iverson. From *Fluxus Codex*. Detroit: Gilbert and Lila Silverman Fluxus Collection, 1988. © Nam June Paik Estate.

Contents

Contents

Revisions: Zen for Film is the tenth Focus Project at the Bard Graduate Center. Topics addressed in the series have been as varied as the interests of the faculty, both permanent and visiting, but this is the first project to address conceptual art of the 1960s. The curator, Hanna B. Hölling, investigates *Zen for Film* (1962–64) by the American artist, born in Korea, Nam June Paik (1932–2006).

Hölling came to the Bard Graduate Center under the auspices of a five-year program generously funded by the Andrew W. Mellon Foundation, Cultures of Conservation, designed to help bridge the gap between the ways objects are studied by conservators and by academics in the human sciences. During her two-year tenure as visiting professor in this program (2013–15), Hölling introduced students to the knowledge created by conservators in her courses, such as "Cultures of Conservation: From Objects to Subjects—On Sites, Rites, and Paradigms" and "In Focus: Beyond the Object Principle: Object—Event—Performance—Process." As a conservator specializing in the conservation of a variety of media who subsequently completed a PhD dissertation on questions of time, identity, and change in Nam June Paik's multimedia installations at the University of Amsterdam, Hölling is particularly well-placed to consider both the practical and the theoretical aspects of conservation in contemporary art practice in film, video, performance, and other recently adopted media. In her final course, given in spring 2015, "In Focus: Revisions—Art, Materiality, and Continuity in Fluxus (1960s–70s)," Hölling turned her attention and that of her students to the peculiar challenges of Paik's *Zen for Film*. *Revisions* is the result of that rigorous examination. The students who participated in this course or acted as assistants and who contributed substantively to the project are Lisa Adang, Cabelle Ahn, Andrew Gardner, Linden Hill, and Lara Schilling.

As Hölling discusses in this publication, the serial creation and exhibition history of *Zen for Film* is extremely complex, leading anyone who explores it to ask about what exactly this work is and where it might be located, whether physically or conceptually or both. The Museum of Modern Art in New York is the only depository of the film relic from the 1960s and of at least three Fluxkit editions of *Zen for Film*. It has generously made a Fluxkit available for exhibition, as well as a film canister that once held the film leader. The original film leader was unfortunately not available for exhibition because of its physical deterioration, which necessitates rigorous preservation in cold storage. We are grateful to Glenn Lowry, the director of the Museum of Modern Art, and Christophe Cherix, the Abby Aldrich Rockefeller Chief Curator of Prints and Illustrated Books, for arranging the loans. David Platzker, curator in the Department of Prints and Illustrated Books, was also involved as loan organizer and interlocutor.

Peter N. Miller, dean of the Bard Graduate Center, sustains the Focus Gallery Project through his fervent support of this collaboration between the Degree

Programs and Research Institute and the Bard Graduate Center Gallery. Elena Pinto Simon, dean of Academic Administration and Student Affairs, provides invaluable advice, as does Nina Stritzler-Levine, director of the gallery. Ivan Gaskell, professor and head of the Focus Gallery Project, oversaw the *Revisions—Zen for Film* project.

Staff members of the Degree Programs and Research Institute and the Bard Graduate Center Gallery collaborated to realize Hölling's ideas: Kate DeWitt, art director; Eric Edler, gallery registrar; Caroline Hannah, acting associate curator; Kimon Keramidas, assistant professor and director of the Digital Media Lab; Marianne Lamonaca, associate gallery director and chief curator; Daniel Lee, director of publishing; Alexis Mucha, manager of rights and reproductions; Stephen Nguyen, exhibition preparator and installation coordinator; Ian Sullivan, exhibition designer; and Ann Marguerite Tartsinis, associate curator and coordinator of the Focus Gallery Project. We are also grateful to Tamara Maletic, Dan Michaelson, and Laurel Schwulst of Linked by Air for developing the vital digital component. The production of this publication was aided by the thorough work of our copyeditor, Carolyn Brown, and proofreader, Christine Gever, as well as diligent report writing by three external scholarly reviewers. I wish to thank these colleagues and all other members of the faculty and staff of the Bard Graduate Center whose thoughtfulness and support made *Revisions* possible.

—Susan Weber
Director and Founder
Iris Horowitz Professor in the History of the Decorative Arts
Bard Graduate Center

Foreword

The curator, Hanna Hölling, has chosen to focus our attention on the early years of conceptual art and its aftermath. In *Revisions*, she shows us a single work—a single work, moreover, that might appear not to be a work at all but rather the very absence of work, for *Zen for Film* by Nam June Paik (1932–2006) is no more than the projection of a loop of transparent film leader, a beam of light streaming through endlessly turning clear cellulose acetate to produce a flickering blank rectangle on a screen or wall. Where anyone might expect to see an image—a moving image—there seems to be nothing. Subtract the image from the projection of movie film and what is left? Nothing? Paik invites us to reconsider. Blankness is a great deal more than we might have assumed. Should we choose to concentrate appropriately on the light thus cast, Paik offers us the opportunity for enlightenment in an unsuspected moment: the moment of *Zen for Film*.

When Dr. Hölling proposed a project entailing the exhibition of just one work, I felt that such a choice could epitomize what the Focus Project is about: concentration. That the work she suggested should be so apparently lacking in physical substance, inviting meditation on absence, unsuspected presence, and even boredom, seemed to me to promise a radical enhancement of the opportunity for concentration. I also anticipated that the obsolescent technology of a clattering film projector might prompt a deceleration of shifts of attention in the viewer together with a prolongation of focus on a seemingly banal ensemble of equipment. I hoped that this might contrast pointedly with the effect of contemporary digital media, which can all too readily elicit insistent impatience in users who expect ever-increasing quantities of information at an ever-faster pace. Only by slowing down can we begin to appreciate that ambience is substance, that absence is unattainable. *Revisions* is in certain respects a distillation of the concept of the Focus Project series in its entirety, as well as a brilliant exposition and analysis of the unplaceable, irreplaceable thing that is *Zen for Film*.

—Ivan Gaskell
Professor of Cultural History and Museum Studies
Curator and Head of the Focus Gallery Project
Bard Graduate Center

Foreword

"What is *Zen for Film*?," I was asked sometime in the early fall of 2014, on the occasion of a preparatory meeting for *Revisions*, an exhibition to feature *Zen for Film* (1962–64), Nam June Paik's "blank" film projection. Despite the many discussions that preceded the meeting, when it came to the question of what the main—and the *only*—artwork of this exhibition was, we felt as if we'd been left in the dark.

Curatorial engagements are not always simple. Only sometimes might they involve the pleasing task of assembling exhibitions from objects that tell fascinating stories. But the act of exhibiting may also fill the space with the vastness of a philosophical challenge, as in the case of *Zen for Film*. The gesture of exposing an artwork to the gaze of the viewer can pose arduous questions—questions with which one struggles without any hope of enlightenment and to which answers are always partial and imperfect. What, then, is *Zen for Film*? If no one asks me, I know what it is. If I wish to explain it to someone else, to paraphrase Saint Augustine, I do not know.

Is *Zen for Film* an object to be respected as an artifact and for its material idiosyncrasies—an object/"multiple" or an object/relic? Is it an idea, a concept—or rather, an event, a performance, or a process? How has what it is been determined by what it once was—or what it has become in the process of reinterpretation? How has it been affected by conceptual and physical change? All in all, *what*, *how*, and *when* is the artwork?

Featuring *Zen for Film* as its main character, this book, *Revisions*, and the exhibition by the same name set out to challenge a number of assumptions about *Zen for Film* from the perspective of its presentation, archivization, and continuation. From such a multifocal stance, and with potential consequences for analogous artworks, *Revisions* addresses what is at stake when it comes to the artwork's presentation—an act shaping not only the (relatively) momentary event of exhibiting objects but also the way in which artworks may be perceived, remembered, and reactivated in the future. Inquiring into the modes of an artwork's existence, *Revisions* observes how technological obsolescence and reinterpretation frame the work's identity. Particularly with respect to recurring installations that undergo the process of de- and re-assemblage, such as *Zen for Film*, questions regarding its institutionalization, display, and distribution become the ones that affect its existence. In the case of iterant artworks, care for the future, a mission long assigned to conservation, is clearly inseparable from the question of curation; reciprocally, curation cannot avoid challenges posed by questions concerning conservation. Conservation, then, like its "object," becomes something else—it considers the continuity of artworks on both a conceptual and a material level rather than fostering attachment exclusively to the material object.

Acknowledgments

The aim of the *Revisions* exhibition and catalogue is to offer a profound understanding of Nam June Paik's filmic work *Zen for Film*. I would like to extend my deep appreciation to Susan Weber, director of the Bard Graduate Center in New York, and Dean Peter N. Miller for their invitation to introduce this hitherto unrepresented topic to the Bard Graduate Center's extraordinary academic forum. This project was made possible through a generous grant from the Andrew W. Mellon Foundation, which supported the Cultures of Conservation curricular initiative and my 2013–15 tenure as an Andrew W. Mellon visiting professor.

I thank Ivan Gaskell, professor, curator, and head of the Focus Gallery Project, for his guiding hand and inspiring discussions from the inception of this project. I am greatly indebted to Nina Stritzler-Levine, director of the Bard Graduate Center Gallery, and her entire team, especially Marianne Lamonaca and Ann Marguerite Tartsinis, for their ever-supportive approach, discussions, and friendship during and beyond this project. I heartily thank Daniel Lee, whose expertise and talent in editorial matters cannot be appreciated enough. I am particularly grateful to Elena Pinto Simon for her insightful criticism and support of the project and to Kimon Keramidas, whose involvement in the development of the digital part of the exhibition and in classroom discussions was crucial. This project benefited from the professionalism and assistance of Kate DeWitt, Eric Edler, Caroline Hannah, Alexis Mucha, Stephen Nguyen, Hue Park, Ian Sullivan, and Han Vu, as well as the support of the Bard Graduate Center Degree Programs and Research Institute staff, Elina Bloch, Keith Condon, and Laura Minsky.

I am deeply grateful to the many faculty colleagues and staff who expressed interest in this project and supported me through discussions about its various stages. I owe a debt of gratitude to David Jaffee and Nicola Sharatt for sharing with me their didactic and curatorial experience in doing exhibitions. Many thanks to Pat Kirkham, Michele Majer, Catherine Whalen, and Paul Stirton for their interest in my research and to Andrew Morrall for being a wonderful neighbor and discussant. Last but not least, I heartily thank Gabrielle Berlinger for her positivity and friendship in and beyond the Cultures of Conservation office.

The aim of the Focus Gallery Project is to conjoin curatorial practice with classroom experience and enable students to gain a profound insight into the processes involved in organizing an exhibition. The Bard Graduate Center students contributed significantly to the development of the project. Lara Schilling, a Bard Graduate Center curatorial fellow, provided invaluable help during every stage of the project. Cabelle Ahn, Andrew Gardner, and Linden Hill, as well as Lisa Adang during an earlier stage, developed preliminary digital media content as well as prototypes. Their keen interest in all matters related to Paik, Fluxus, and intermedia, as well as challenges and criticism in and beyond the classroom, make teaching a source of genuine pleasure. One of the delights of my activity at the

Acknowledgments

Bard Graduate Center was the collaboration with MA and PhD students, Antonia Behan, Martina D'Amato, Hadley Jensen, Jaimie Luria, Summer Olsen, and Ariel Rosenblum. They have contributed to my thinking in many ways, and I owe them a great deal. I thank Kirstin Purtich for her help proofreading the manuscript.

I am indebted to chief curator Christophe Cherix and the curatorial, registrar, and conservation teams of the Museum of Modern Art in New York for the effort it invested in lending *Zen for Film* and its multiple components, as well as to Jon Huffman, Nam June Paik estate curator, for his support in this endeavor. I thank David Platzker for sustained discussions about the loan. I also thank him, Jim Coddington, and Kim Conaty of the Museum of Modern Art in New York for the opportunity to collaborate on the "Fluxus Listening Project," an ongoing initiative at the Museum of Modern Art Silverman Archives in Queens, New York, that exposes the characteristics of Fluxus audio recordings in continuous negotiations between analogue and digital formats. For fruitful discussions, I am most grateful to the MoMA Fluxus team, including Katherine Alcauskas, Sydney Briggs, Kim Conaty, and Kate Lewis.

My deep gratitude goes to Jon Hendricks, whose most profound knowledge of Fluxus is a continuing source of inspiration. I thank Barbara London for many inspiring discussions and for sharing her unique experiences with me. I would like to thank Jonas Mekas for his insights into the avant-garde of the 1960s and his patience in answering my numerous questions both in person and by email. I am also indebted to Michael Century for his musicological inspiration and friendship, to Lori Zippay for stimulating conversations about Electronic Arts Intermix collections and Fluxus anthologies, and to Mona Jimenez for linking me with Bill Brand, to whom I owe a debt of gratitude for sharing his invaluable insights as an artist and archivist working with (experimental) film. For discussions and support of my research, I am indebted to Andrew Lampert and John Klacsmann of the Anthology Film Archives in New York. As this project extends my earlier work, I also thank the vast number of people who have granted me the most generous support during my research in a dozen countries on three continents and whose ideas and activities informed this book. I regret I cannot name them all here.

I heartily thank Sarah Cook and the anonymous reviewers for providing me with their valuable comments and suggestions. I would also like to acknowledge the editorial help of Clare Donald, Carolyn Brown, and Christine Gever. I am grateful to Barbara Burn for editing the exhibition didactics. Thanks also to Dan Michaelson and Laurel Schwulst of Linked by Air for their development of the digital component of the exhibition.

Deborah Cherry and Glenn Wharton offered tremendous support with their wisdom and friendship during part of this project at an earlier stage. To Jonny Hedinger, my debts are deeper than I can ever acknowledge.

Introduction

Overture

Positioned against the backdrop of a white rectangle, the silhouette of a man casts a sharp-edged shadow on its surface (fig. 1). The borders of the rectangle are markedly soft and irregular, which, in the era of digital perfection, signifies some distant time, lost to the past—a time when film projectors reified cinematic representation. The figure is Nam June Paik, whose image and shadow were captured when he was a young Korean artist, aged 33, who had already gained some attention. The image shows Paik turned away from the camera lens, as if he were deliberately engaging with the theatrical shadow play, an ancient precinematic tradition, uninterested in the potential audience. The image reveals Paik's silhouette cut above his knees, his body facing the white rectangle. One is tempted to believe that the photograph's perspectival distortion, balanced by the weight of Paik's reflection, is an effect of contingency rather than a carefully considered photographic staging. This photograph, taken by Peter Moore, a passionate photographer of the New York art scene, became an iconic representation of *Zen for Film*. In a clear and effective gesture, Moore's photograph seized not only a singular moment of Paik's life but also of his film.

This unusual portrayal of Paik staring at, and featuring in, his artwork conjures the potential for multivalent ways of engaging with *Zen for Film*—looking and seeing, beholding, participating and grasping. It also indicates its documentary quality—as a record and, simultaneously, as a leftover from *Zen for Film*'s performance, valued even more for its rarity. Turned away, but even more present as amplified through the assumed reflection, compelling through its stillness, and evoking connotations, Paik's contemplative posture becomes our posture. Throughout this book, we will assume this posture while approaching what only at the beginning might appear crystal clear—a film that projects its own filmic materiality on the flatness of a screenlike surface. But beware of its deceptive simplicity. Following Paik, I am inviting you—whether a reader or an exhibition visitor—to *look at* and *through* the artwork, questioning its material and conceptual status and revisiting any preconceived and established points of view.

The Film

Zen for Film as featured in Moore's photograph is part of a rather sparse photographic archive that provides evidence of the artwork's early development. Moore took this image during the New Cinema Festival I, Film-Makers' Cinematheque, in New York on November 2, 1965.[1] Jonas Mekas, director of the Cinematheque and champion of the underground film community, commented: "I realized . . . when I watched Nam June Paik's evening [at the Cinematheque] . . . his art, like the art of La Monte Young, or that of Stan Brakhage, or Gregory Markopoulos, or Jack Smith, or even (no doubt about it) Andy Warhol, is governed by the same thousand year

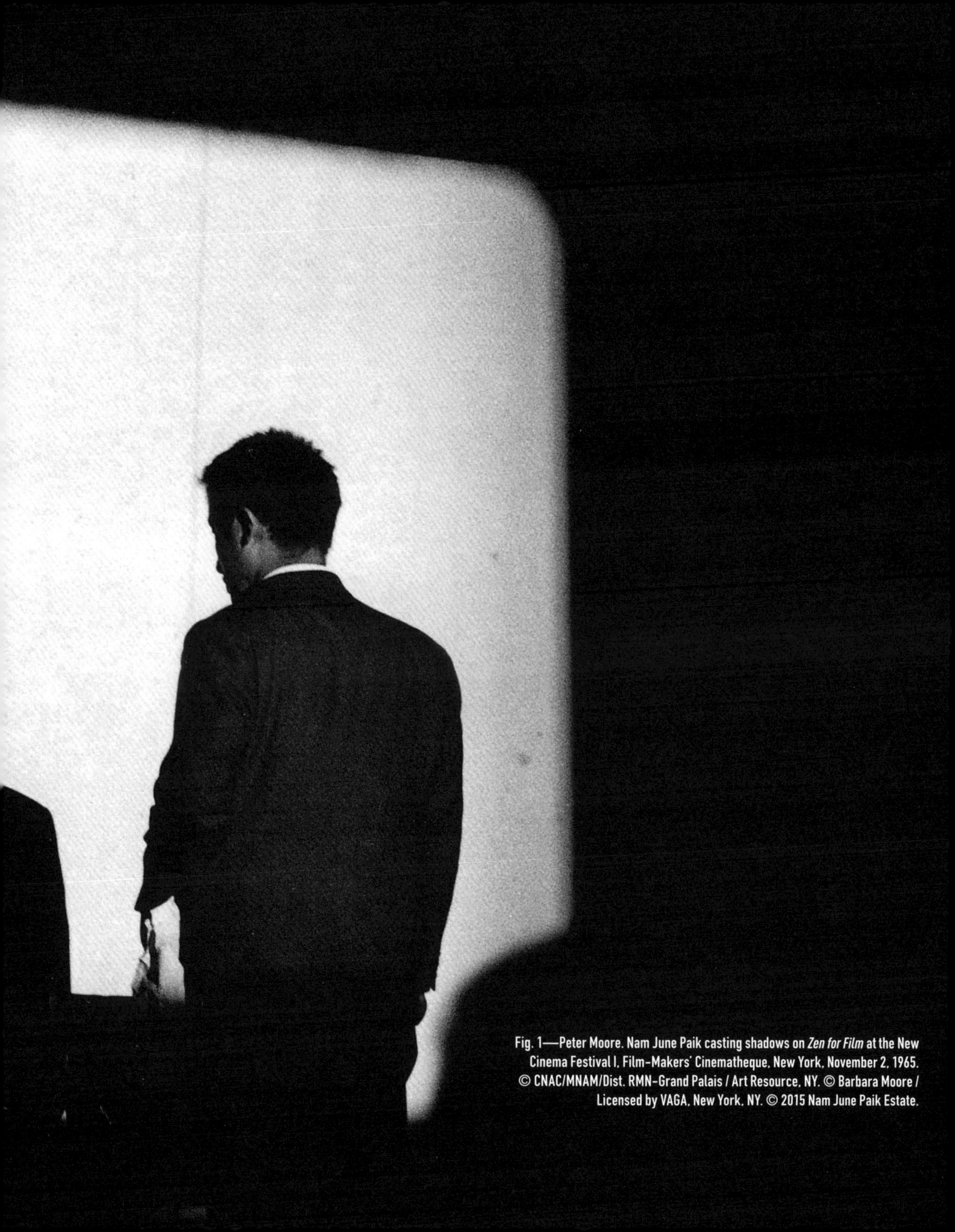

Fig. 1—Peter Moore. Nam June Paik casting shadows on *Zen for Film* at the New Cinema Festival I, Film-Makers' Cinematheque, New York, November 2, 1965.

old aesthetic laws and can be analyzed and experienced like any other classical work of art."[2] Paik, he added, "did away with the image itself, where the light becomes the image."[3]

An earlier, lesser-known photograph from Moore's estate presents us with a snapshot revealing a home movie atmosphere (fig. 2). This image was taken during an early screening of *Zen for Film* at an event staged in May of 1964, as part of the influential six-week Fluxus festival at the Fluxhall on Canal Street in New York City, to which Paik was invited by George Maciunas. According to film historian Bruce Jenkins, during the presentation at the Fluxhall, Paik's film barely filled "half of a home movie-sized screen that was positioned at the front of the loft space adjacent to an upright piano and a double bass."[4] Stripped to the projecting apparatus and film stock itself, *Zen for Film* was, in a sense, an antifilm that, in a performative gesture—and similar to John Cage's idea of "no sound" music—exposed its own material conditions, accompanied by the rattling mechanics of the projector.

Despite the significance of *Zen for Film*'s material qualities as an analogue film projection that, in a sense, turns the innards of a cinematic apparatus outward and exposes the commonly unexposed to the viewer, reconstructing its early appearance exactly presents difficulties. For the most part, as I will show, this is a result of the scarcity of sources and varying specifications regarding the length and type of the film stock, as well as the duration and type of the projection (looped or linear). Sources fail to indicate the type of projector that was used for the screening—perhaps a sign of insufficient attention paid to the materiality of the apparatus in art historical accounts in general. Theories of visuality have, for a long time now, abandoned interest in materiality other than on an abstract, general level.[5] In contrast to the many documented manifestations of *Zen for Film* in various galleries in the recent past, the early images neither record the presence of the projector within the frame of their composition nor take notice of the viewer of the spectacle, with the notable exception of Moore's 1965 photograph featuring Paik in a double role: as viewer and as maker.

—

The history of the emergence of *Zen for Film* might be contextualized within the development of avant-garde cinema and also independent film and video. It must be noted, however, that, despite certain overlaps of the world of video and performance artists of the 1960s and 1970s within the domain of experimental filmmakers, it is only in the following decades that the two separate realms become intertwined.[6] One reason why these two artistic cultures of making were so decidedly distant from each other might be seen in the overly distinct materiality of

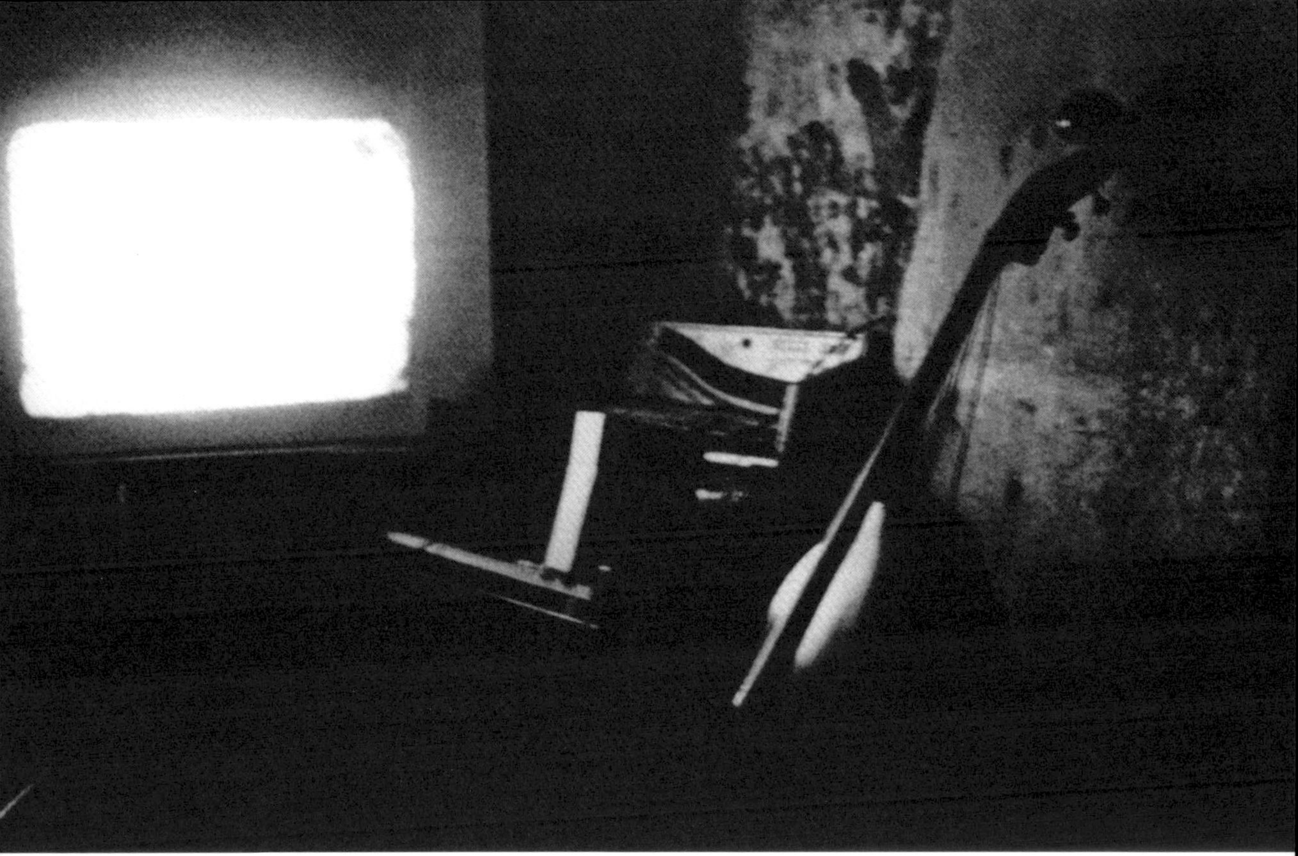

Fig. 2—Peter Moore. *Zen for Film* during a Fluxus festival at Fluxhall, New York, 1964.

film and video, the individual paths of development of film and video and their divergent historical roots (from the point of view of the technology of representation, film was a successor to photography, whereas video was a new technical format altogether), the logic of the recording and playback devices (immediacy of video versus delay through film processing), and the temporal specificity of the media. Video and performance artists placed themselves against the historical development of the visual arts and the art historical paradigm in general, while the filmmakers developed their strategies by contradicting the established forms of filmmaking and the film industry.[7]

Inspired by European experimental film, including Surrealist and Dadaist works,[8] experimental and independent filmmaking began in America in the 1940s. In New York, Jonas Mekas, a Lithuanian émigré based in America, paid critical attention to experimental cinema. Not only did he found New York Cinematheque and organize the New Cinema Festival I,[9] he also founded *Film Culture*, an avant-garde cinema magazine, to which Maciunas, the "Fluxus impresario," contributed as a designer.[10] The Cinematheque became a happening place of active participation and interaction of visual and performance artists, where new uses of cinema—new techniques, forms, and subjects—began to flourish.[11] It was also where Paik presented his blank film and where Moore shot his most evocative photograph.

Fluxus artists characteristically combined multiple genres and media. Paik, in his creative practice, worked with filmmakers, video artists, performers, musicians, and television and broadcast professionals. His use of media transgresses common assumptions not only about media purity but also about a progressive succession of formats. For instance, in Jud Yalkut and Paik's *Electronic Moon* (1966–69), Paik's earlier work *Moon Is the Oldest TV* (1965), which was a manipulation of multiple television monitors, is transferred to 16mm film. By inverting the media genealogy, the electronic visualization again becomes a photogram, a single film frame,[12] while the temporal structure of film distances itself even further from video and television.

The idea of *Zen for Film* must have emerged during the time Paik was working on his groundbreaking exhibition in Wuppertal, Germany, the *Exposition of Music–Electronic Television* (March 11–20, 1963), which largely employed manipulated TV monitors in a participatory event, conjoining Paik's musical inclination with experiments in visual arts and technology. Conforming to his inversion of media genealogy, in *Zen for Film* Paik returned, if only for a short time, to the analogue medium after he had already explored the possibilities of the electronic image. Therefore, reflecting the zeitgeist and resistant to easy or pleasing classifications and attributions, *Zen for Film* occupies a space in between cinema and performing arts, music (or sound art) and visual imagery, anticipating the temporal dynamics of "intermedia," a term that Dick Higgins introduced and that the

Norwegian scholar Ina Blom also uses to describe artistic activities, such as visual poetry and performance art, that dissolve boundaries between various genres and media, and between art and life.[13] *Zen for Film* is invested as well in questions of space, locating itself in direct relation to the emerging genre of installation art.

Through the radical break with the figurative image—or any kind of visual representation—and by drawing attention to the production process and material aspects of its own technical-aesthetic infrastructure, *Zen for Film* is linked with structural film, represented by artists such as Tony Conrad, Hollis Frampton, Peter Kubelka, Paul Sharits, and Michael Snow. In contrast to politically engaged cinema, structural film emphasizes the material aspects of the film medium, revolving around the qualities of both the film itself and the film apparatus.[14] Structural films are both objects and processes, at times completed, at times functioning as unfinished fragments.[15] Rather than exposing the viewer to the narrative encounter of a documentary or fictive story or to any kind of filmic imagery in a representational sense, the structural film is colored, cut, and manipulated, reflective of its own materiality, and concerned with duration and its own temporal unfolding.[16] "The CONTENT carried by film," according to Kubelka, "is linked inseparably to the MATERIAL OBJECT. Film, like any other medium, can only be fully understood in its ORIGINAL FORM."[17]

A significant step toward these new aesthetics—and perhaps the most immediate context for *Zen for Film*—Fluxus films (Fluxfilms) were short statements about film that renounced any creative transformation of the material in the conventional sense.[18] Fluxfilms emerged as a result of Maciunas's cinephilia and his interest in film culture and humor.[19] His enthusiasm for expanding Fluxus activities into the area of cinema had an impact on Fluxus's creative output.[20] By apparently returning to the proto-cinematic experiments of Eadweard Muybridge and reinventing them within the context of mass production, Maciunas, through Fluxfilm, ostensibly wished to uncover what remained buried under the Hollywood-dominated mode of filmmaking.[21] It would be wrong, however, to refer to Fluxfilm as a nostalgic return to the cinematic past or an exercise in abandoning narrative. Rather, the project of Fluxfilm, in which reflexive aspects are enacted on a material as opposed to narrative level, addresses contemporaneity. Fluxfilm manipulates technological apparatus (not as a production machine but as a potentiality in itself) while implementing a good portion of humor (at times corrosive). Fluxfilm isolates the movements of its own film leader as it passes through the projector (Maciunas's *Ten Feet*, 1966) or of the filmed subject (Yoko Ono's *Number 4* sequence of moving buttocks, 1966), slows down the motion by manipulating the cinematic apparatus and re-recording the image, or exemplifies the medium's temporal passing simply by accumulating dust, as in *Zen for Film*. Whereas the authorship of individual films remains attributed to the artists of Fluxus's expanded circle, the initial idea and mode of production of Fluxfilms must be ascribed entirely to Maciunas.

The principal compilation of Fluxfilms can be found in different editions of *Flux Year Box 2*[22] (ca. 1968; fig. 3), comprised of 8mm film loops by artists including Paul Sharits, Eric Andersen, John Cale, John Cavanaugh, Maciunas, Robert Watts, Yoko Ono, and Wolf Vostell.[23] This compilation of "special items-works," including a hand-crank film viewer for an immediate appreciation of the films, was conceived of as a continuation of the idea of a yearbox—an encyclopedic-anthological Fluxus "sammelsurium," to be spread through Fluxus's distribution system in the United States, Japan, and Europe. Although *Zen for Film* seems to be absent from *Flux Year Box 2*, it was distributed as part of a number of variants of collective Fluxkits, such as "Flux-Kit ('A' copy)" (unique copy, 1965; fig. 4) and "Flux-Kit ('B' copy)" (1965; fig. 5), listed in *Fluxus Etc.*[24]

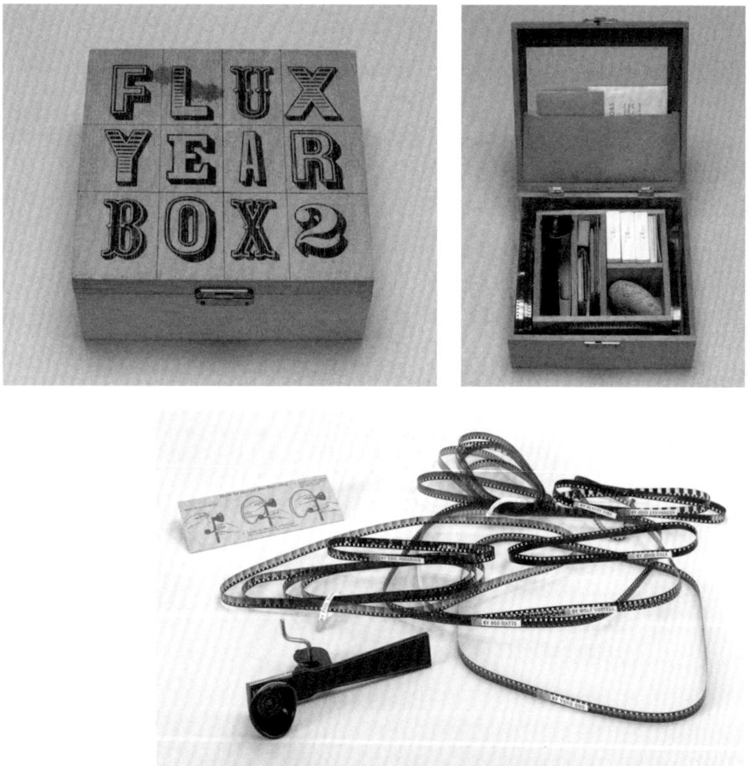

Fig. 3—*Flux Year Box 2*, ca. 1968. Fluxus Edition announced 1965. Designed and assembled by George Maciunas. Top: Wood box containing objects in various media, with screenprint, metal clasp, and hinges. Bottom: Film loops with cut-and-pasted paper, metal and plastic viewer, and offset card. The Museum of Modern Art, The Gilbert and Lila Silverman Fluxus Collection Gift, 2460.2008.1–26. © The Museum of Modern Art / Licensed by SCALA / Art Resource, NY.

In addition to yearboxes and Fluxkits, Maciunas also produced discrete "packages" of Fluxfilms rendered on separate prints, which he revised multiple times and distributed internationally as part of Fluxus programs (fig. 6).[25] Featuring varying lengths and compilations of Fluxfilm works, these programs were at times accompanied by music.[26] Occasionally, in the vein of *Expanded Cinema* and challenging the traditional idea of film projection, Maciunas envisioned the film screenings in a specially designed environment that included multiple film projections and the viewer's participation.[27] Although reduced to a simple projection placed in a specific space, I believe that this experiential aspect, reinforced by the multisensorial character of the film installation, is also intrinsic to *Zen for Film*.[28]

Regardless of the film's looped or linear character, Maciunas's film packages compiled the otherwise individual films sequentially, the order varying depending on the compilation. The films were announced by titles—"FLUX FILM NO. [number]"—flashing consecutively in large black or white letters on a white or black background.[29] Maciunas approached the design of the title sequences creatively, by adjusting their formal design, rhythm, or structure, or by introducing a significant feature so that the style of the titles would refer to the content of the film. The credits often included the name of the artist, a copyright notice, and a note crediting a cameraman.

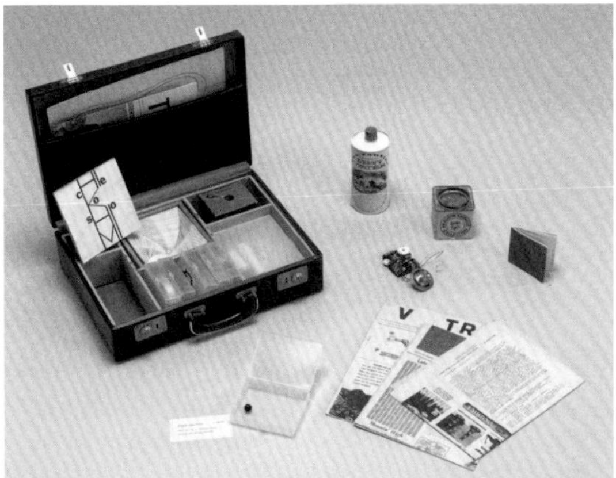

Fig. 4—*Fluxkit (A copy)*, 1965. Fluxus Edition. Vinyl-covered attaché case, containing objects in various media. Assembled by George Maciunas. Containing objects by: Ay-O, George Brecht, Dick Higgins, Joe Jones, Alison Knowles, Takehisa Kosugi, Nam June Paik, Benjamin Patterson, Mieko Shiomi, Ben Vautier, Robert Watts, Emmett Williams, and La Monte Young. The Museum of Modern Art, The Gilbert and Lila Silverman Fluxus Collection Gift, 2426.2008.1-1-21. © The Museum of Modern Art / Licensed by SCALA / Art Resource, NY.

Zen for Film—Fluxfilm No. 1 opens the *Fluxfilm Anthology*, believed to have been created by Maciunas sometime between 1962 and 1970.[30] *Fluxfilm Anthology* compiles films by, among others, George Brecht, Maciunas, Ono, Paik, Sharits, Mieko Shiomi, Ben Vautier, Vostell, and Watts, ranging from ten seconds to ten minutes in length. Some of the projections were conceived of as continuous loops, while others were linear documentaries taking as subject matter the events and happenings of the 1960s New York avant-garde. Frequent references in *Fluxus Codex*—Hendricks's comprehensive compilation of Fluxus objects and materials from the 1960s through 1978—suggests 1966 as a starting point for Maciunas's assemblage and distribution of "film programs," with the anthology perhaps as one of them. It remains unclear, however, whether these programs were meant to function as autonomous pieces (they were offered for rent and later for sale), curatorial projects, festival presentations, or all of these.[31] According to *Fluxus Codex*, *Zen for Film* began to be included in Fluxfilm programs starting in 1970.[32]

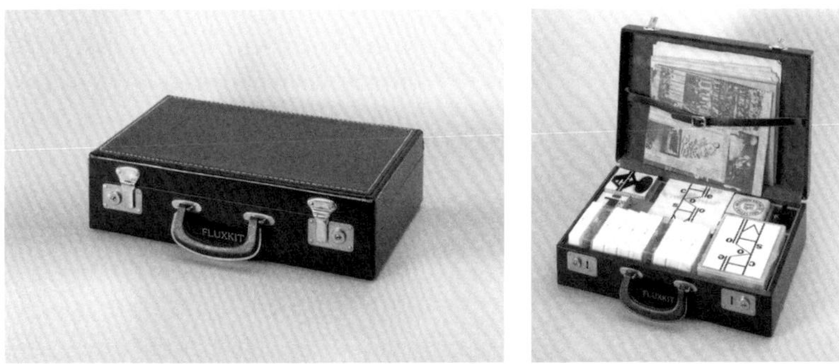

Fig. 5—*Fluxkit (B copy)*, 1965. Fluxus Editions, announced 1964. Vinyl-covered attaché case, containing objects in various media. Assembled by George Maciunas. Containing objects by: Eric Andersen, Ay-O, George Brecht, Dick Higgins, Joe Jones, Alison Knowles, Takehisa Kosugi, George Maciunas, Nam June Paik, Benjamin Patterson, Mieko Shiomi, Ben Vautier, and Robert Watts. The Museum of Modern Art, The Gilbert and Lila Silverman Fluxus Collection Gift, 2182.2008.1-28. © The Museum of Modern Art / Licensed by SCALA / Art Resource, NY.

Zen for Film—Fluxfilm No. 1 from *Fluxfilm Anthology* consists of a title sequence, "FLUX FILM 1 ZEN FOR FILM BY NAM JUNE PAIK,"

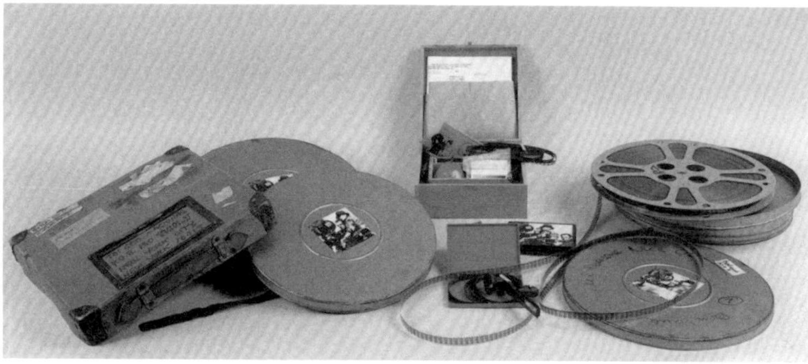

Fig. 6—Various artists. Fluxfilms programs compiled on 16mm loops; packagings of Fluxfilm Loops and a Flux Year Box 2 containing Fluxfilms Loops. Photograph by Brad Iverson. From *Fluxus Codex*. Detroit: Gilbert and Lila Silverman Fluxus Collection, 1988. © Nam June Paik Estate.

followed by a little less than eight minutes of an almost blank image. Although the white letters on a black background show signs of deterioration, the virtually white image that follows seems to contain, proportionally, only a few smudges and particles.[33]

Fluxfilm Anthology exists in at least two roughly 2-hour versions of thirty-seven and forty-one films and a related 40-minute film program.[34] Anthology Film Archives in New York City holds the *Fluxfilm Anthology* compilation of thirty-seven films (the completion of which some sources ascribe to Mekas in 1992).[35] The location of the initial 16mm footage of *Zen for Film—Fluxfilm No. 1*, together with other separate works that came to constitute *Fluxfilm Anthology*, is unclear.[36] A digital file of the thirty-seven-film variant of *Fluxfilm Anthology*, originating from a VHS tape acquired through *Re:voir*, can also be found in the collection of Electronic Arts Intermix (EAI) in New York.[37]

The Artist

> [Paik] is small, short, I mean, smaller than Toshi, but hair not too short but growing straight up, like a field of wheat. Walks around all winter in sandals and a scarf wound right to his eyes. Calls nearly everyone Hallo, Hallo, Hallo when he has something to say. He is very modest and unpretentious which is in great contrast to many people here in N.Y. In fact he is not eager to perform or have his work performed at all, which is even more unusual. He speaks English and German like Japanese, so very few can understand him at first. He is extremely friendly.
>
> —Letter from George Maciunas to Dick Higgins, January 18, 1962

Nam June Paik (fig. 7) is one of the most fascinating figures of the neo-avant-garde. Born in Seoul, in what is now South Korea, Paik immigrated fairly early on to Hong Kong and later to Japan, escaping the Korean War and returning to his country of birth only decades later. At the University of Tokyo, he studied music, aesthetics, and art history, read Hegel in German, and focused his musicology thesis on Arnold Schoenberg. He made Germany his European home and remained attached to it through his professorship at the Kunstakademie

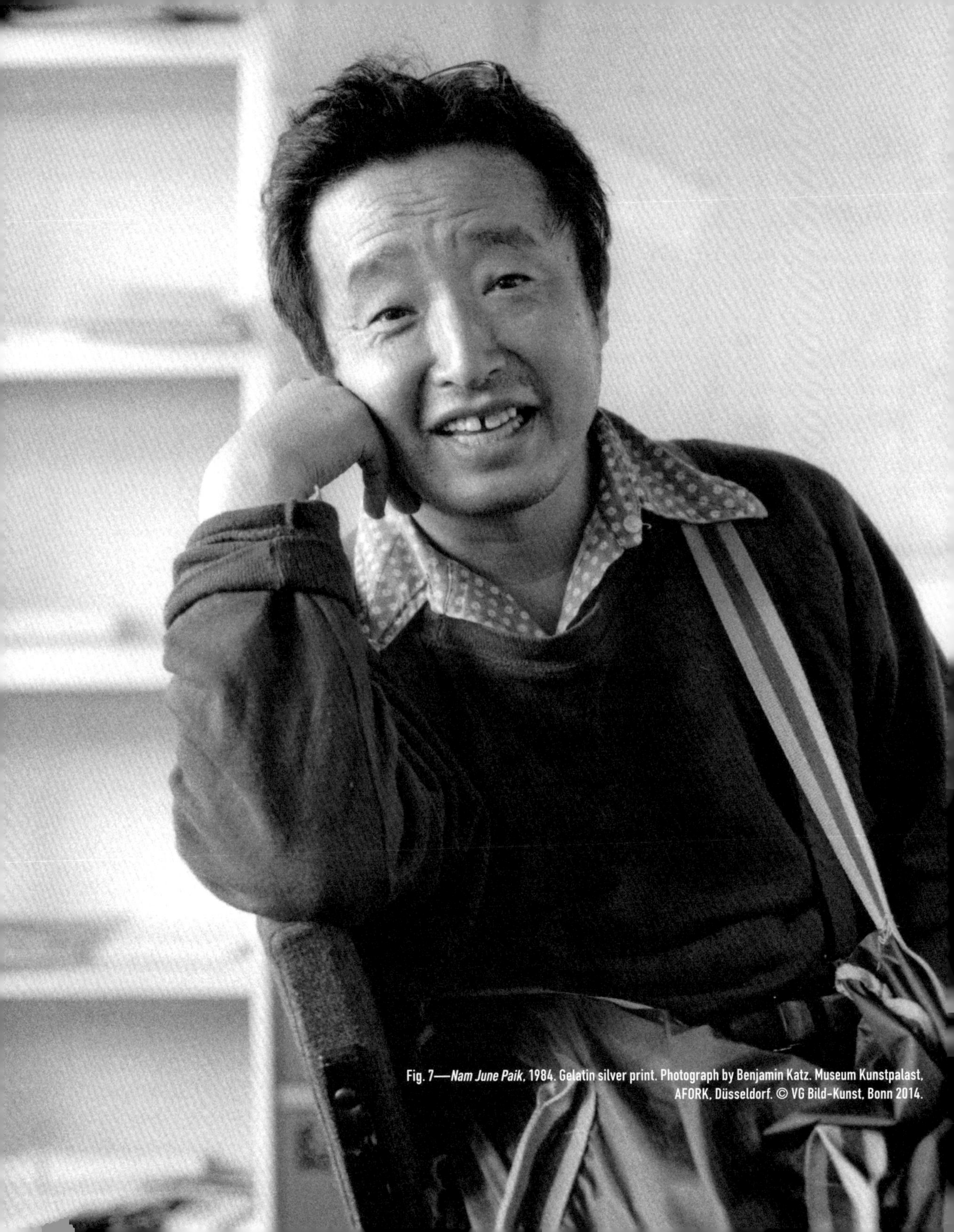

Fig. 7—*Nam June Paik*, 1984. Gelatin silver print. Photograph by Benjamin Katz. Museum Kunstpalast, AFORK, Düsseldorf.

Düsseldorf even after he moved to New York City.[38] Although Wolfgang Fortner was his teacher in Freiburg, on Fortner's advice Paik migrated to Cologne to work in the electronic studio of the West German radio station WDR, a hub of avant-garde progressive musical activity. The intellectuals and artists in the immediate circle of Karlheinz Stockhausen and Mary Bauermeister—with Bauermeister's atelier as a center of artistic events—became a hugely influential environment for Paik. Artistic action, literature and music, and film and electronic experiments in the field of acoustics, with its endless potentiality for manipulation, came together in the search for a new *Gesamtkunstwerk*, or "total artwork."[39] For Paik, his encounter with Stockhausen and Cage had already taken place during summer school courses for new music in Darmstadt. Although Stockhausen's role in the development of Paik's creative practice should not be underestimated, Cage and the interdisciplinary advances in music, including the elements of chance, indeterminacy, and Zen philosophy, continued to have an impact on Paik. At the Galerie Parnass in Wuppertal, over the course of several days in March 1963, Paik mounted the influential exhibition for the development of electronic media, television, and video, *Exposition of Music–Electronic Television*. He might have conceived of *Zen for Film* sometime while preparing the Wuppertal exhibition.

Paik exhibited considerable versatility throughout his long artistic career. From single video works through megalithic video walls and multimonitor installations, robotic experiments and video synthesizers, satellite projects and performances, Paik proved to be one of the most prolific (and celebrated) multimedia artists of the second half of the twentieth century.[40] Rather than being driven purely by the mystical traditions of the East, Paik moved among cultures, traditions, trends, sentiments, and attitudes—a true cultural nomad with charisma and an extraordinary ability to inspire.

One of the distinctive features of Paik's work is rooted in Marcel Duchamp's and Cage's modernisms, expressed by the use of found objects, the technique of bricolage, action and performance, and the guiding principles of chance and randomness. Although Paik's openness toward new technologies became his signature, the ironic side of his deployment of technology and love of "antitechnological technology" are often forgotten.[41] Inspirational to generations of makers and curators, Paik's pronouncement that "as the collage technique replaced oil-paint, the cathode ray tube will replace the canvas" remains valid, notwithstanding the continued rise and rapid obsolescence of new forms of media and technology.[42] The rise of digital technology has made Paik's immensely rich creative output highly relevant for the many inquiries into the status of media, as well as their reinterpretation and transition, authorship, curation, and dissemination, including questions regarding art and culture in general.

Fluxus in the Time of the 1960s

In 1961, Paik met George Maciunas and began his engagement with Fluxus's evolving ideology. Although a number of Paik's artworks and activities responded to the spirit of Fluxus and were presented in this context, as in the case of other Fluxus "participants," it is difficult to determine exactly whether Fluxus modified Paik's creative output or merely offered what might only be identified in retrospect as a conceptual-temporal framework for his creative project.

But what exactly was—or is—Fluxus?[43] Fluxus (from the Latin word meaning "flow") has been interpreted as "the most radical and experimental art movement of the sixties" (Harry Ruhé) and, in contrast, as "a wild-goose chase into the zone of everything ephemeral" (Henry Martin).[44] More a state of mind than an art movement and notoriously impossible to define,[45] Fluxus was an international forum of artists, composers, and designers centered around—at least in its 1962–78 phase—Maciunas, who was an organizing force for the movement. Fluxus engaged in blending art forms, media, and disciplines in the 1960s and 1970s.[46] Rather than characterizing it in terms of a uniform style or attitude, Fluxus might best be conceived of as a platform for certain activities as well as for the distribution and publicity of artworks.[47] Maciunas chose the word "Fluxus" first as the title for a Lithuanian cultural club magazine, but in 1961 it became the title for the planned issues of a Fluxus magazine related to art.[48] Fluxus artists continually sought to rename the group. But the kind of work produced by Fluxus existed before its expansion and would continue after Maciunas's death—a point of closure, though disputed, for a large number of the group's activities. In 1962, Fluxus was not a "new art movement" but rather a tendency that followed from various sources. Fluxus aimed to destroy the boundaries between art and life, and, much in keeping with the social climate of the 1960s, to make art (and art making) available to everybody. Fluxus endeavored to overturn the elitist bourgeois character of high art. "Everybody can be [an] artist. Everybody should be," proclaimed Fluxus artist Robert Filliou.[49]

With its roots in Dada, Fluxus propagated "do-it-yourself" aesthetics in a prolific way while valuing simplicity over complexity.[50] Fluxus operated somewhere between the performing and the visual arts, implementing a variety of expressive means, such as film, painting, sculpture, poetry, electronic media (including video and television), performance, happening, and event.[51] Events, with their short "scores," new music, Fluxus boxes, and editions, belong to the diversity of Fluxus's creative output. The origins of Fluxus lie in the concepts of indeterminacy and experimental music that Cage explored in the 1950s.[52] Beginning in 1956, Cage's teaching at the New School for Social Research in New York had an enormous influence on a number of attending artists, including George

Brecht, Al Hansen, Dick Higgins, Allan Kaprow, and Jackson Mac Low. Equally important for Fluxus's crystallization were the 1958 international summer school courses for new music in Darmstadt, where Paik and others learned about the latest interdisciplinary advances in music.[53]

In Cologne, a series of events organized by Bauermeister in her atelier at Lintgasse 28 spawned what is often described as Proto-Fluxus.[54] Its circle of participants included visual artists, composers, architects, and avant-garde poets such as Joseph Beuys, Cage, Arthur C. Caspari, Christo, Hans G. Helms, Mauricio Kagel, David Tudor, Vostell, Stefen Wewerka, and Paik himself. Additionally, the artistic network centered on Stockhausen's electronic studios at WDR in Cologne is considered to be the European antecedent to Fluxus in America. Such beginnings also determined Fluxus's musical inclinations and much of its performative and performed character.[55] Although they have not been sufficiently emphasized in art historical discourse, Fluxus's musical roots and the development of notation, score, and instruction-based logic can claim a significant place in the development of conceptual tendencies of the 1960s.[56] This basis in experimental and avant-garde music rather than in the visual arts and the difficulty of documenting early performances, along with the anti-art character of Fluxus, its independent system of distribution, and its inherent internationalism, may be why Fluxus's formative influences on other movements remained underappreciated for so long or simply lacked recognition altogether.[57]

Notwithstanding others' cultivation of Fluxus theories, the project of determining the direction of Fluxus in its early years should be credited to Maciunas. His manifestos, charts, "learning machines,"[58] and art historical clarifications positioned Fluxus in a broader visual and performing arts culture.[59] The ideas of Fluxus are connected with the radicalism of the 1960s and Maciunas's idealism and utopian vision, including his sympathy for concretism (which emphasized the concrete reality of objects independent of representation or symbolism) and the ready-made. His visionary perspective is manifest in his encouragement to "purge the world of dead art, . . . abstract art, illusionistic art."[60]

Fluxus became a well-established network of distribution overseen and controlled by Maciunas. Numerous Fluxus concerts and festivals were "organized," as Maciunas put it, to promote and sell "whatever we were going to produce."[61] The *Conditions for Performing Fluxus Published Compositions, Films and Tapes*, which Maciunas established, determined when a concert should be designated as a Fluxconcert and an artwork designated as a FluxPiece, accompanied, no doubt, by the appropriate permissions and fees. Most important for their afterlives, however, is the characteristic manner in which the series of concerts and festivals came to be assembled in the Gilbert and Lila Silverman Fluxus Collection, as overseen by Jon Hendricks.[62] Its original archival system was dictated by the order of appearance of events in which the works occurred rather than their authorship (often multiple authors or a Fluxus collective) or genre, which, as I have noted, is difficult to establish. After its acquisition of the Silverman Fluxus Collection in 2008, MoMA had to reorganize the original assemblage of materials to comply with its own classification structures. The rearchiving and reorganizing of the Silverman collection is but one of many examples of an organically assembled system of idiosyncratic documents and artworks that refuse to be easily corralled by standardized museum cataloging systems.[63]

—

Fluxus, like much of the art of the 1960s, engaged directly with the subject of time. It is in this context that *Zen for Film* emerged. Artworks created during the early part of this epochal decade are marked by their involvement in aspects of time and temporality, contingency, and chance. The endless repetition of installations evoked a certain timelessness. The simultaneity of their existence in time, their circularity and automatization, and the seriality of their materialization are manifest not only in Paik's artworks but also in those of Carl Andre, Donald Judd, Sol LeWitt, and Lawrence Weiner. The idea of a work produced according to a set of instructions to a certain degree enabled artworks to "overcome time" in that it secured their repeatability.[64]

In *Of Other Spaces* (1986) Michel Foucault points out that "we are in the epoch of simultaneity: we are in the epoch of juxtaposition, the epoch of the near and far, of the side-by-side, of the dispersed. We are at a moment."[65] Introducing "chronophobia," a neologism signifying our insistent struggle with time, Pamela Lee characterizes the 1960s as accelerated, anticipatory, and repetitive, marked by the endlessness of historical reckoning and endlessness as a cultural phenomenon.[66] The acceleration of life in all aspects created a distinct perception of time. In response, artists, curators, and activists of the 1960s attempted to give form to time's changing conditions, to still its acceleration or master its passage. The sixties' love of technology and its applications for artistic ends not only came with a different understanding of processed time but opened up the possibilities of an indefinite creative processing of time, discernible, as we will see, in Paik's *Zen for Film*.

The Rationale behind Revisions

Curatorial tasks are often tied to making exhibitions—displaying artworks in a space according to a meaningful concept.[67] *Revisions*, to a degree, subverts this idea. By presenting *Zen for Film*'s manifestations and explicating its condition, this Focus Gallery Project questions what the artwork is and what it has become through its life and through the course of its many distributions, displays, and manipulations. *Zen for Film*'s projection, the film remnant from the 1960s, Fluxus editions, and Fluxprograms problematize its existence. Therefore, the intentions behind *Revisions* are not concerned purely with exhibiting objects, nor do I aim simply at evoking a minimal aesthetic of display, undoubtedly attractive in other contexts. Indeed, *Revisions* strives to unfold the world of an artwork without any potential disruptions, exposing the artwork as artwork—the "thing" and its world, its event, and its process.

The rationale behind this project is to critically revise—and question—some assumptions about *Zen for Film* so as to foster a broader reflection not only about media that refuse simple classifications but also about artworks radically shaped by curatorial, conservation, and presentation decisions. With no ambition to exhaust the potential of such an approach, and leaving the space for further inquiries open, *Revisions* focuses on what usually remains hidden behind the façade of aesthetic and narrative content—an intertwined coalescence of materiality and visuality in permanent flux, a changeable source of equally changeable meaning.

The word "revision" derives from the Latin *revisio*, which means "seeing again."[68] Its synonyms include emendation, correction, alteration, adaptation, editing, rewriting, and redrafting. In British English, "to revise" often means "to reread" or "to study," as for an exam.[69] Hence, I propose to revisit the artwork and its world from a wide-ranging perspective, taking on art historical, theoretical, and philosophical strands to account for the multiplicity of interpretations, contingencies of meaning, and possibilities of change in *Zen for Film*.

In these pages, which offer an extended analysis of *Zen for Film*, I have constructed a sequence of thematically ordered chapters, or "revisions," spanning a theoretical-historical context and the frameworks of exhibition, dissemination, and continuation. I begin the revisions that follow by presenting three encounters with *Zen for Film* that problematize its multifaceted existence. I then explore the ideas of nothingness, boredom, and Zen Buddhism involved in Paik's artwork in revision 2, in preparation for tackling in revision 3 the issue of cinematic time so intriguingly destabilized by *Zen for Film*. Its multiple existence as film, editions, and object is the focus of revision 4. Revision 5 is devoted to its museum and exhibition life. From this consideration, I continue in the remaining revisions with an inquiry into *Zen for Film*'s associations with music, conceptual art, and performance, as well as the associated aspects of authenticity, authorship, and intention. I conclude with a proposition for understanding *Zen for Film* in terms of relative duration.

This cross-disciplinary inquiry into *Zen for Film* has been triggered by the premise that if we are to continue maintaining responsibility for the lives of artworks, we—scholars, curators, conservators, and caretakers—must understand profoundly *what* they are. The act of revising, or looking again, in the following chapters should serve this purpose.

Notes

Portions of *Revisions—Zen for Film,* particularly revisions 1 and 3, draw on my earlier research, "*Re*:Paik: On Time, Changeability and Identity in the Conservation of Nam June Paik Multimedia Installations" (PhD diss., University of Amsterdam, 2013). Its revised version, *Paik's Virtual Archive: Time, Change, and Materiality in Media Art,* in preparation for publication by the University of California Press, is a tribute to Nam June Paik. Like *Revisions,* the forthcoming book is written for anyone fascinated by the enchanted materiality of Paik's oeuvre and the intellectual challenge posed by the physical and conceptual continuation of his works. But rather than drawing strategies for the future, this book addresses the present. "The future"—posits Paik—"is now."

1—See Hanhardt, *The Worlds of Nam June Paik,* 75.

2—Mekas, *Movie Journal,* 210, quoted in Hanhardt, *The Worlds,* 82.

3—Ibid.

4—Bruce Jenkins gives May 8, 1964, as the date of the first public screening of *Zen for Film.* Jenkins, "Fluxfilm in Three False Starts," 68. Jon Hendricks alludes instead, in his anthology of Fluxus events and materials, to a number of earlier screenings. Hendricks, *Fluxus Etc.*; hereafter cited as *Fluxus Etc.* George Maciunas dates *Zen for Film* to 1962–64. Maciunas, "Some Comments on Structural Film," 349.

5—On the abandonment of interests in materiality, see Elkins, "On Some Limits of Materiality in Art History," 25–30.

6—This became apparent in work by artists such as Douglas Gordon and Stan Douglas in the 1990s. See Eamon, "An Art of Temporality," 74.

7—Ibid. It is important to note that film and video cultures diverged at the institutional as well as the individual artistic level. With the exception of a few specialized institutions, experimental cinema tends to gain less attention in both traditional art museums and film archives. This has a direct effect on the reception and afterlife of experimental films. The two strands of evolution of the "moving image" refer, on the one hand, to video works collected in small numbers as "fine art" in museums and galleries, and, on the other hand, to the lack of understanding on the part of visual arts museums about experimental or avant-garde film. See Iles and Huldisch, "Keeping Time," 65–83.

8—Among the influential films were Luis Buñuel's *Un Chien Andalou* (1929), Fernand Leger's *Ballet Mécanique* (1924), and Marcel Duchamp's *Anémic Cinéma* (1926).

9—The New Cinema Festival I was later known as the Expanded Cinema Festival, most prominently associated with Gene Youngblood. His book *Expanded Cinema* (1970), discussing various forms of new technology, considers video as an art form.

10—See Ganz, "An Introduction to the Fluxfilm," 6. Maciunas had a very close relationship with Mekas. Notoriously without money, Maciunas lived in the basement of Mekas's Film-Makers' Cinematheque on Wooster Street. According to art historian Thomas Kellein, from late 1963 onward, Maciunas typed Mekas's *Film Culture* on his IBM Executive, which offered at least a partial solution to his financial problems. Kellein, *The Dream of Fluxus,* 87.

11—Mekas' Cinematheque cannot be associated with just one place, however, as it had multiple venues.

12—Subversion of artistic structures was characteristic of Fluxus. In Vostell's Fluxfilms (*Sun in Your Head,* Fluxfilm no. 23, 1963) the 8mm-film camera videotapes material from television programs. Rush, *Video Art,* 69.

13—Higgins sought inspiration in Duchamp's blurring of media boundaries and valued continuity over categorization. See Higgins, "Statement on Intermedia." Intermedia created a way of operating that provides an alternative to the fixed categories of art. They enabled, as Ina Blom puts it, an understanding of the material in terms of its own conditions. Blom, "The Intermedia Dynamic: An Aspect of Fluxus." Although indirectly, the concept also anticipates what later came to be called "new media." For a comprehensive elaboration of the new media with respect to their curation and preservation, see Graham and Cook, *Rethinking Curating.*

14—Although many artists worked with this type of film before the 1960s, the term "structural film" derives from P. Adams Sitney's article "Structural Film," originally published in *Film Culture,* no. 47 (Summer 1969), in which he identifies stuctural film as "a cinema of structure wherein the shape of the whole film is predetermined and simplified, and it is that shape that is the primal impression of the film." For a discussion of structural film and Maciunas's rebuttal of Sitney's article, as well as a chart depicting Fluxus's relation to structural film, see Sitney, "Structural Film," 349.

15—For structural film, see Peter Gidal, ed., *Structural Film Anthology.*

16—This formalist attitude was criticized in the troubled 1960s—the period of the Vietnam War and escalating political conflicts. The counterpart of this movement might be seen, among others, in European alternative cinema by Peter Weibel, Otto Muehl, Kurt Kren, and Valie Export.

17—Kubelka, "Peter Kubelka: Filmmaker," 92. Original capitalization.

18—See Hein, "On Structural Studies," 114.

19—Maciunas adopted the term "Fluxfilm" around 1965, at a time when he began producing a sufficient number of films to be able to plan a two-hour program. See Jon Hendricks, *Fluxus Codex*, 63; hereafter cited as *Fluxus Codex.*

20—See Ganz, "An Introduction," 4.

21—See Saper, "Fluxus as Laboratory," 143.

22—See *Fluxus Codex*, 122–23.

23—See ibid., 122–24.

24—See *Fluxus Etc.*, 102. *Fluxus Etc.* terminology differs from *Fluxus Codex*, which uses "Fluxkit" rather than "Flux-Kit." I have chosen to maintain the original spelling when I refer to versions from these resources.

25—According to Jim Ganz, as early as 1964, and with only two films at his disposal—Paik's *Zen for Film* and Dick Higgins's *Invocation of Canyons and Boulders for Stan Brakhage*—Maciunas envisioned a Fluxus film festival. Ganz, "An Introduction," 3.

26—See letter from Maciunas to Friedman, November 14, 1966. *Fluxus Codex*, 60.

27—"A booth must be set up in a fairly dark area, the walls of which are of white vinyl or cotton sheets (about 12 ft. wide) hanging as curtains and creating a room 12 ft. × 12 ft. or smaller. Four 8mm loop projectors (with wide angle lenses) must be set up, one in front of each wall (on the outside) and projecting an image, the frame of which is to cover the entire wall. 20 sets of loops are available. Visitors, a few at a time, must enter this booth to observe the film environment around them." "Proposed Fluxshow for Gallery 669, Los Angeles. Opening Nov. 26, 1968," in Hendricks, ed., *Fluxus Etc. / Addenda I*, 193; hereafter cited as *Addenda I.* For the idea of a film and sound capsule and a related concept of implementing Fluxfilms as "wallpaper," see *Fluxus Codex*, 64–65.

28—Because it reconfigures the space in which it is installed, *Zen for Film* also carries the characteristics of installation art. It not only *presents* rather than represents the light and mechanics of the projector, the texture and dust of the film, it also addresses the viewer directly as a presence in an immersive environment through which and as which the work is rendered complete.

29—See Ganz, "An Introduction," 3. See also "Fluxus Project Planned for 1967," quoted in *Fluxus Codex,* 61.

30—The date 1962–70 for *Fluxfilm Anthology* seems to be rather tentative and might point to the creation of the individual films as well as the anthology. As in the case of all Fluxfilm programs, Paik's involvement in the creation of the *Zen for Film* print included in the anthology remains unclear. Mekas maintains that all films were conceived of as separate pieces and compiled by Maciunas into the anthology for convenience. Mekas (artist, filmmaker), in discussion with the author, February 2015.

31—"This fall, we . . . intend to visit Prague. . . . We could bring with us . . . a 2 hour film program of some 15 films." Maciunas to Milan Knizak, possibly January 1966, *Fluxus Codex*, 59. "Incidentally, loops from these films will go into Fluxus II Yearboxes." Maciunas to Vautier, March 29, 1966. *Fluxus Codex*, 123.

32—*Zen for Film* opens the list in 1970 ("Nam June Paik [Zen for Film]") and is second to last on a list from 1974: FLUXFILMS, 1974 VERSION ("1. Nam June Paik. ZEN FOR FILM 1964. Clear film, accumulating in time dust and scratches") in "FLUXFILMS, 1974 VERSION," *Fluxus Codex*, 63. It must be noted that neither the short 40-minute nor the long 75-minute version of Fluxfilms from 1966 credited to Moore (camera) and Maciunas (editing and titles) includes *Zen for Film*. *Fluxus Codex*, 60–61.

33—My assessment of *Zen for Film—Fluxfilm No. 1* concerns a film print that I was able to view at the Anthology Film Archives.

34—Mekas, discussion with the author.

35—Although four films (nos. 32–35) are missing according to the brochure "Fluxfest: In and around Fluxus" (1992) and information retrieved on the Gartenberg Media Enterprises and Stendhal Gallery websites, the Anthology Film Archives holding is the most complete version of a series that Maciunas began to gather in 1966. "Fluxfest: In and around Fluxus"; Gartenberg Media, "Fluxfilm Anthology," accessed March 10, 2015, http://www.gartenbergmedia.com/dvd/fluxus.html; Stendhal Gallery, "Fluxfilm Anthology," accessed March 10, 2015, http://stendhalgallery.com/?page_id=1490.

36—Although a note on the website of Anthology Film Archives lists "Flux Film Anthology—41 separate works (1960s–70s) at John Allen Lab (c. 1993)," it is difficult to retrieve the materials because the archive is not publicly available. Therefore, oral interviews with Mekas, curators, archivists, and preservationists remain an invaluable (in fact, the only) source of research. Anthology Film Archives conducted a substantial preservation of *Fluxfilm Anthology* in the 1990s, and its copy, which I was able to view during my research, also stems from this time. Andrew Lampert (curator of collections, Anthology Film Archives), in discussion with the author, March 2015; John Klacsmann (archivist, Anthology Film Archives), in discussion with the author, March 2015.

37—EAI lacks a master of *Fluxfilm Anthology*—evidence of the compilation's complicated existence and perhaps also a reason for EAI's limiting access to the digitized file of *Fluxfilm Anthology* to educational use. However, as of June 2015, EAI ended their relationship with *Re:voir* and are now working directly with Anthology Film Archives. Another variant of *Fluxfilm Anthology* can be found at the Film-Makers' Coop, which distributes *Fluxfilm Anthology* as a 2-hour DVD. Additionally, the Film-Makers' Coop holds a 40-minute Fluxfilm program on 16mm film, which includes sixteen Fluxfilms, but not *Zen for Film*. For the EAI holding, see Electronic Arts Intermix, "Fluxfilm Anthology," accessed December 25, 2014, http://www.eai.org/title.htm?id=11976. Lorri Zippay (director of the Electronic Arts Intermix), in discussion with the author, March and June 2015. For the Film-Makers' Coop holdings, see http://film-makerscoop.com/rentals-sales/search-results?fmc_authorLast=fluxus&fmc_title=&fmc_description=&x=0&y=0. Light Cone, a French organization devoted to the distribution, promotion, and preservation of experimental film, holds both variants of *Fluxfilm Anthology* on four 16mm reels.

38—Paik was awarded the position as the first professorship in video in Europe in 1979.

39—The attempt to create *Gesamtkunstwerk* is not exclusive to this artistic milieu. On the other side of the globe, Allan Kaprow engaged in extending the possibilities of art making. See Kaprow, "Notes on the Creation of a Total Art," 5–6.

40—Paik's prolific productivity as media artist secured a permanent position for his oeuvre in public and private collections. And yet it is striking that, until recently, research into the materiality and changeability of his works that goes deeper than the basic material level (usually concerning the replacement of old playback and display technology with new) has been lacking.

41—Paik, in an interview with Russell Connor, 1975.

42—See Foster, Krauss, Bois, and Buchloh, *Art since 1900*, 561.

43—For Fluxus-related monographs and publications that inspired this publication, see Baas, *Fluxus and the Essential Questions of Life*; Block, *1962 Wiesbaden Fluxus 1982*; Friedman, *The Fluxus Reader*; Kellein, *Fluxus*; Ruhé, *Fluxus*.

44—Quoted in Phillpot's preface to Phillpot and Hendricks, *Fluxus*, 7.

45—See Anderson, "Fluxus: Early Years and Close Correspondences," 7. According to Tobias Berger, "anyone who tries to define Fluxus knows nothing about it." Block and Berger, "What Is Fluxus?," 38.

46—As direct contact with living Fluxus artists is becoming increasingly rare, Fluxus, as we know it, is often "learned" from a number of publications that, as Block puts it, portray only a certain aspect of Fluxus, often limited to geographical or intellectual spheres. See Block and Berger, "What Is Fluxus?," 39.

47—See Owen Smith, "Developing a Fluxable Forum," and Dick Higgins, "Fluxus: Theory and Reception," 3–21, 217–36.

48—See Phillpot, "Fluxus: Magazines, Manifestos, *Multum in Parvo*," in Fluxus, 9.

49—Filliou, "GOOD-FOR-NOTHING-GOOD-FOR-EVERYTHING (c. 1962)," 854.

50—Maciunas's first presentation in Europe at the Parnass Gallery in 1962 was titled "Neo-Dada in den Vereinigten Staaten" (Neo-Dada in the United States). See Becher and Vostell, *Happenings, Fluxus, Pop Art, Nouveau Réalisme*.

51—To be exact, the event and event score were "invented" by Fluxus.

52—Multiple authors refer to Cage's inextricability from the emergence of Fluxus. See Decker, *Paik Video*, 182; Schüppenhauer, *Fluxus Virus*, 11. Cage himself was aware of his centrality to Fluxus. See Daniels, "Vier Fragen an John Cage," 214.

53—See Wulf Herzogenrath, "When the Future Was Now: Wulf Herzogenrath on Nam June Paik," *Tate ETC.*, accessed December 23, 2012, http://www.tate.org.uk/tateetc/issue21/namjunepaik.htm.

54—See Dörstel, Steinberg, and Zahn, "The Bauermeister Studio," 56–67.

55—Some scholars even refer to Fluxus artists as "composers." Knapstein, "Fluxus," 86.

56—In his essay "Concept Art," Henry Flynt states: "'Concept art' is first of all an art of which the material is 'concepts,' as the material of . . . music is sound. Since 'concepts' are closely bound up with language, concept art is a kind of art of which the material is language." Flynt, "Concept Art," n.p. Maciunas's *Expanded Arts Diagram* (1968) (in Eric Crosby, introduction to *Art Expanded, 1958–1978,* Walker Art Center, http://www.walkerart.org/collections/publications/art-expanded/introduction/, accessed April 26, 2015) credits Flynt with formulating his thoughts as early as the 1950s. It should be noted, however, that Flynt's proposition was not meant to be representative of the condition of art in general (Kosuth); rather, it was a strategy of the depletion of art. See Osborne, *Conceptual Art,* 19.

57—Osborne, *Conceptual Art*, 19.

58—For a discussion of "learning machines," see Schmidt-Burkhardt, *Maciunas' Learning Machines.*

59—For Maciunas's philosophy of Fluxus and situating it in a broader culture, see, for instance, "Transcript of the Videotaped Interview with George Maciunas by Larry Miller, March 24, 1978," in *Addenda I*, 10–28; hereafter cited as "Transcript of Maciunas Interview."

60—Phillpot, "Fluxus, Magazines, Manifestos, *Multum in Parvo*," 11.

61—"Transcript of Maciunas Interview," 15.

62—The Gilbert and Lila Silverman Fluxus Collection is considered one of the largest and most significant worldwide. Its beginnings might be traced back to about 1977, when Gilbert Silverman, real-estate developer and art connoisseur, started collecting Fluxus with the help of Jon Hendricks, proprietor of a store called Backworks (together with Barbara Moore). Hendricks introduced Silverman and his wife to the movement, helped them to collect Fluxus material, and authored several essential resources on Fluxus. The Silverman collection was acquired by MoMA in 2008. See MoMA, "The Gilbert and Lila Silverman Fluxus Collection Archives in the Museum of Modern Art Archives," 2013, accessed December 12, 2014, http://www.moma.org/learn/resources/archives/EAD/Fluxusf.

63—See Michelle Elligott, Miki Kaneda, Julia Pelta Feldman, and Gretchen Wagner, "Archival Workshop at MoMA," *Post: Notes on Modern and Contemporary Art around the Globe* (blog), February 15, 2013, http://post.at.moma.org/content_items/153-archival-workshop-at-moma.

64—See Hölling, "*Re*:Paik," 65–70.

65—Foucault, "Of Other Spaces," 22.

66—See Lee, *Chronophobia.*

67—See Hoffman, *Ten Fundamental Questions of Curating*, 15.

68—To "revise" is to "look at again, visit again, look back on." *Online Etymology Dictionary*, s.v. "revision," "revise," accessed December 15, 2014, http://www.etymonline.com/index.php?term=revise&allowed_in_frame=0.

69—I thank Daniel Lee of Bard Graduate Center for suggesting the British English meaning of the word.

"Anyway, if you see my TV,
please, see it more than 30 minutes."
—Nam June Paik

Revisions

1st Revision—

Encounters

No. 1

In a slightly darkened gallery, I am standing in front of a white screen that fills a rectangular wall with a proportional cinematic rectangle. The image appears to blur toward the edges, its contour soft, its corners slightly curved. The film projector clatters relentlessly, transporting a filmstrip through its inner mechanism, pushing its plastic body tooth by tooth through perforations—a rather monotone, yet persistently present, mechanical "soundtrack." The machine is located on a pedestal slightly below my eye level; I feel the warmth it produces. The shutter interrupts the emitted light during the time the film is advanced to the next frame, unnoticeable but somewhat palpable. The projected image is almost clear and, at first sight, static. I am attending the event, standing inert, without any expectation of an image appearing—I have experienced such an event before. Time elapses. On the screen of my imagination the whiteness delineates Paik's black silhouette on the white background of this projection, from fifty years ago. In the next take Jean-Luc Godard projects his imaginary pictures on the same blank screen. Thinking about the physiology of viewing the film, I am trying to imagine how—in the perceptual process of my brain and on my retina—the image remains, evoking an illusion of motion rather than an observation of singular frames. Yet nothing happens. I am observing the whiteness. I close my eyes and see a black negative of the projected surface. I am back to vision. People pass by, and in some sense being able to register nonverbal cues, I register their skepticism. Their shadows move away from the projected image unnoticed, effaced. I keep my view engaged on the whiteness. This contemplation plays out, gradually, when I realize that the whiteness, rather than showing nothing, contains random information—dark traces of different kinds appearing occasionally: smudges, particles, shadows. The eyes, the brain—I think—are somewhat trained to overlook this evidence of film's materiality. It occurs to me that the longer my observation endures, the more I can see, the more that appears on the initially very hygienic projection. On the abstract bright "canvas" of the image vertical smudges emerge: hairs, blurry grayish stains. In staccato, the image darkens and lightens slightly following the mechanical motion of the projector. I am drawn to its physicality, the audio of its mechanical processes of display, the sober intensity of non-illusory real time, and the way in which it imposes contemplation and requires engaged spectatorship before it reveals itself.

No. 2

A white cubic space right behind the passage from one part of an exhibition to another is illuminated by a perfectly bright rectangular image. I hardly noticed the entrance while passing through noisy displays and being overrun by various impressions of flickering, visual richness. I enter the room. I stand still. I wait. Nothing happens. Beethoven's *Moonlight Sonata* enters the space from the neighboring video installation (perhaps Paik's *Global Groove*). The image projected in front of me is white, perfectly rectangular, showing regular, sharply cut edges. It seems to just *exist*, unaffected by anything happening around it or anyone in the room, a white flag of pristine image. Slowly, somewhere from behind, the unobtrusive humming presence of a digital projector becomes recognizable. As I turn away from the image toward the source of the light, I can see the projector located right below the ceiling in the upper center of the wall. I sit down on a chair situated beneath the projector. I sit and wait. My eyes hurt from the whiteness. The word "hospitality" appears in my mind. I sense hospitality in the way I was received in this room, on that chair, but I also register the uncanny impression of being in a place ruled by emptiness and hygienic precaution—a hospital. I can hear lively sounds from behind the walls, a world reserved for somewhere or something else, and I am haunted by an unfulfilled desire to hear and see more, which becomes an unbearable disruption.

No. 3

I bend over to view a round film can in a vitrine at an exhibition. The can is slightly open, concealing a roll of transparent film stock—barely recognizable. For a while I observe it, studying its dimensions and form, the stains of oxidation on the can's lid and some traces of tape once applied. The film itself is not "clearly" visible. I recall an online image depicting a similar can and three boxes with film leaders, apparently replacements for the loop wound on the reel. It occurs to me, all of a sudden, that there is hardly any difference between this film presented in front of me in a sealed museum vitrine and the virtual version of a photographic image delivered from a server somewhere. Both are distant, both deactivated, both a potentiality rather than an actuality. Still, gazing at the object behind the glass, I attempt to project this film onto the apparatus of my imagination and guess what it contains. What would it reveal if I were able to view it? I imagine the sound accompanying the projection and myself inspecting the projecting device in a position that would enable me to see the full image and its source at the same time. Yet the film I am looking at is still, somewhat useless, enclosed twofold in the can and in the museum vitrine—a sign of its valuable and exceptional status. I am able neither to view it nor to smell it. It is isolated from me and from the surrounding exhibition—still and static, an artifact or relic, one part of an unknown whole, a stagnant remnant of an unfulfilled spectacle.

—

The encounters with *Zen for Film* open up the question of what the artwork is in relation to the change it has experienced. What happens to the artwork's identity if we face its presentation and conservation—an experience, an object, a projection, or a relic, or perhaps all of these—simultaneously? They also open up the aspect of changeability that pushes the limits of what can be understood as still the same object, and when it becomes something else. Can a work of art invite change by its very nature? The different methods of exhibiting *Zen for Film* also raise the question of how curation—as a strategy of presenting the artwork to the viewer that goes hand in hand with conservation—may influence the work's changeability by the choice of a particular technology. They also question how an artwork functions within a certain historical moment when the availability of technology dictates its aesthetic qualities, and, in the same vein, when this technology changes, following the unstoppable progress of its development.

Describing the three episodes of viewing *Zen for Film* evokes impressions for me that match three different encounters with this work. The first is with *Zen for Film* (analogue film loop, film projector), exhibited in the show *Bild für Bild—Film und zeitgenössische Kunst* at the Museum Ostwall, Dortmunder U, in Dortmund, Germany, December 12, 2010–April 25, 2011 (fig. 8). The second, with a digital video projection (8 min., loop), takes place at the exhibition *Nam June Paik: Video Artist, Performance Artist, Composer and Visionary* at Tate Liverpool, England, December 17, 2010–March 13, 2011 (fig. 9). And the third, *Zen for Film* (canned film reel), occurs at the exhibition *The Third Mind: American Artists Contemplate Asia, 1860–1989* at the Guggenheim Museum, New York, January 30–April 19, 2009 (fig. 10).[1] The three forms of *Zen for Film* could not be more different from one another: the first is a filmic projection; the second, a digital projection; and the third, a film reel. And yet they claim to be *Zen for Film*—the same work of art. In *Revisions*, I strive to reconstruct the conditions of some of these encounters.

Zen for Film at Museum Ostwall, on loan from the Centre Pompidou in Paris, consisted of a filmstrip (a loop) run through a film projector. Resembling closely the early concept of *Zen for Film* from the Fluxhall festival, the artwork

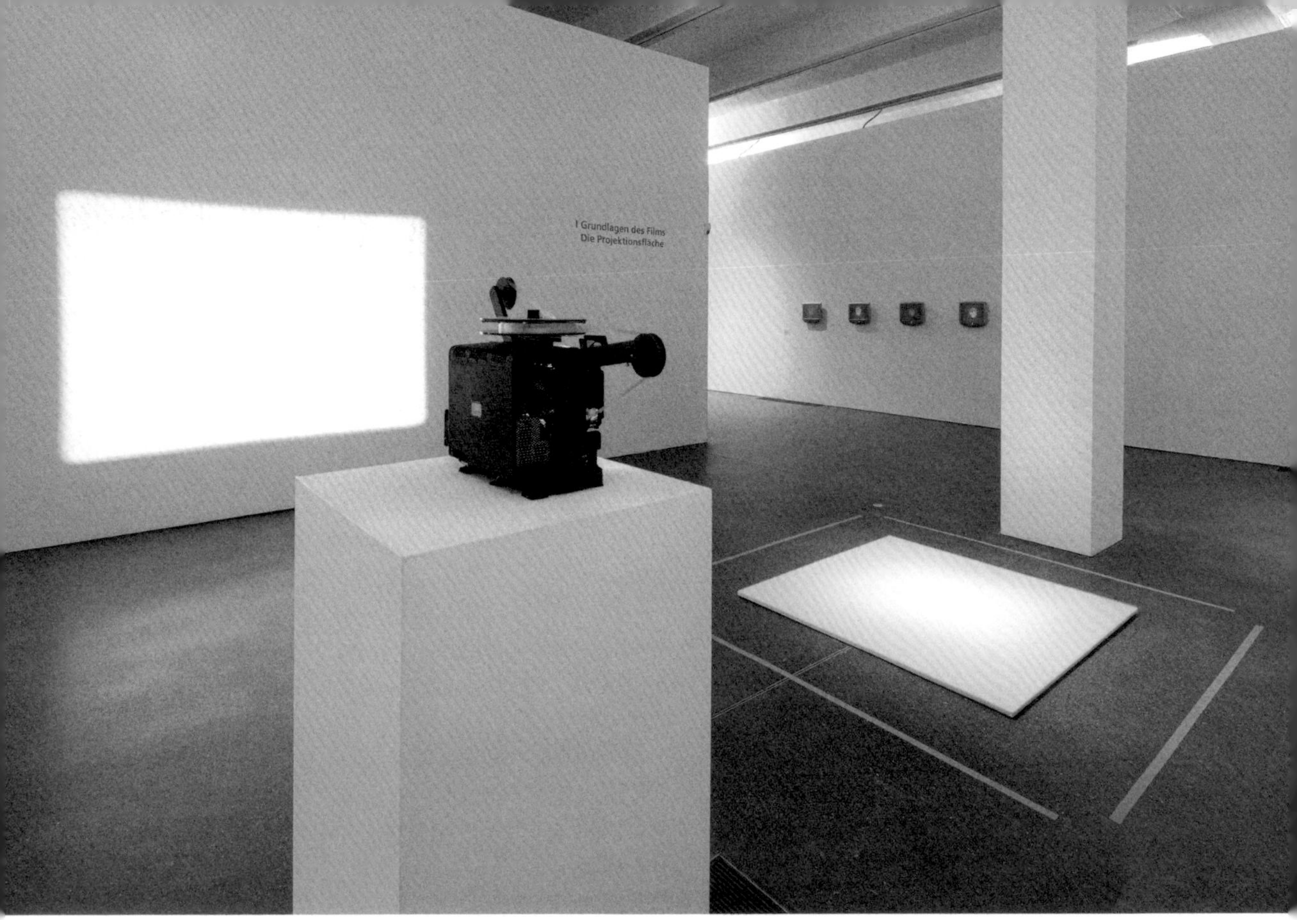

Fig. 8—*Zen for Film* installation in *Bild für Bild—Film und zeitgenössische Kunst*. Museum Ostwall, Dortmunder U, Dortmund, Germany, December 12, 2010–April 25, 2011. Photograph by Jürgen Spiler. Museum Ostwall im Dortmunder U, Dortmund, Germany.

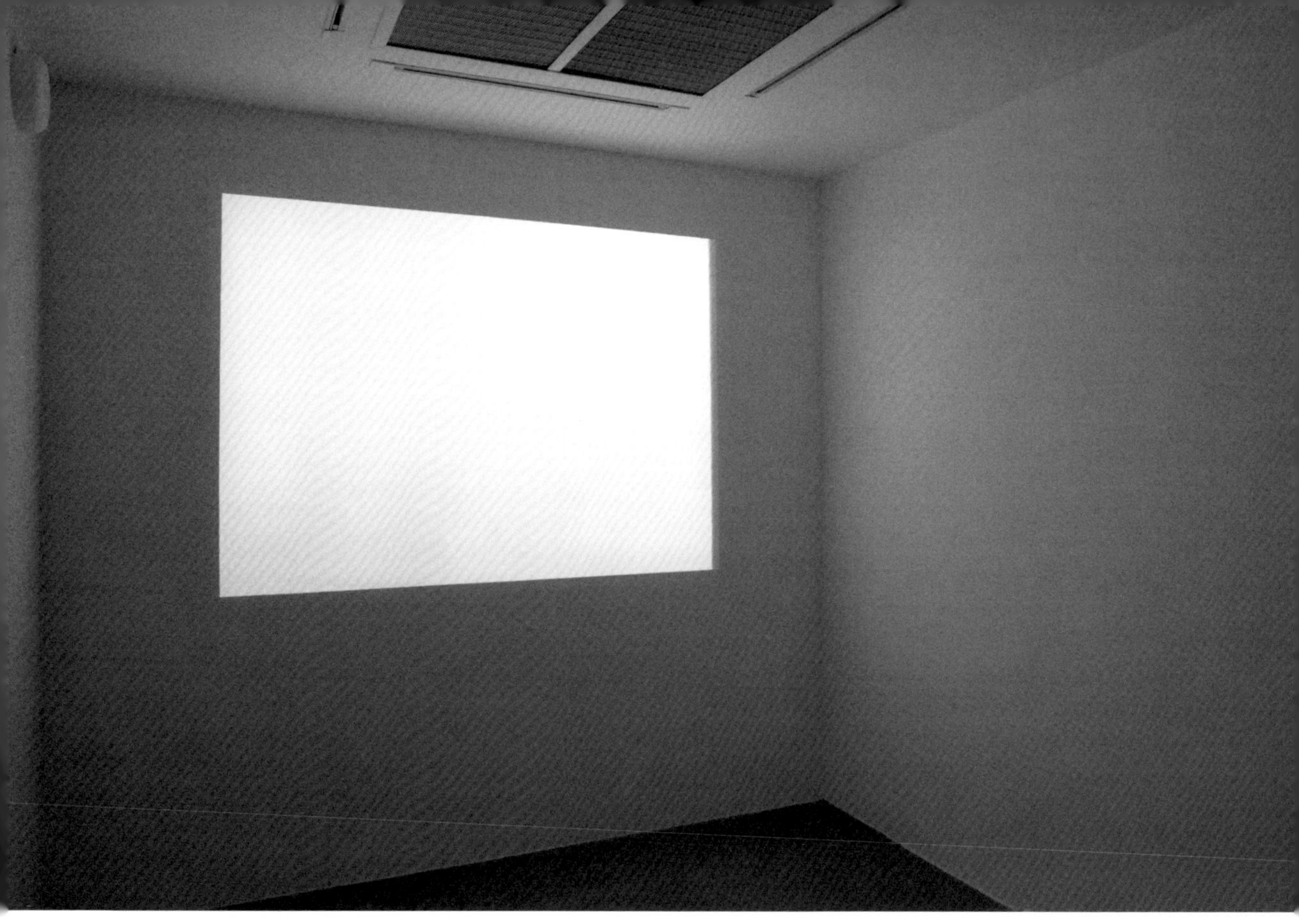

Fig. 9—*Zen for Film* installation in *Nam June Paik: Video Artist, Performance Artist, Composer and Visionary*. Tate Liverpool, December 17, 2010–March 13, 2011. © Tate, London 2015.

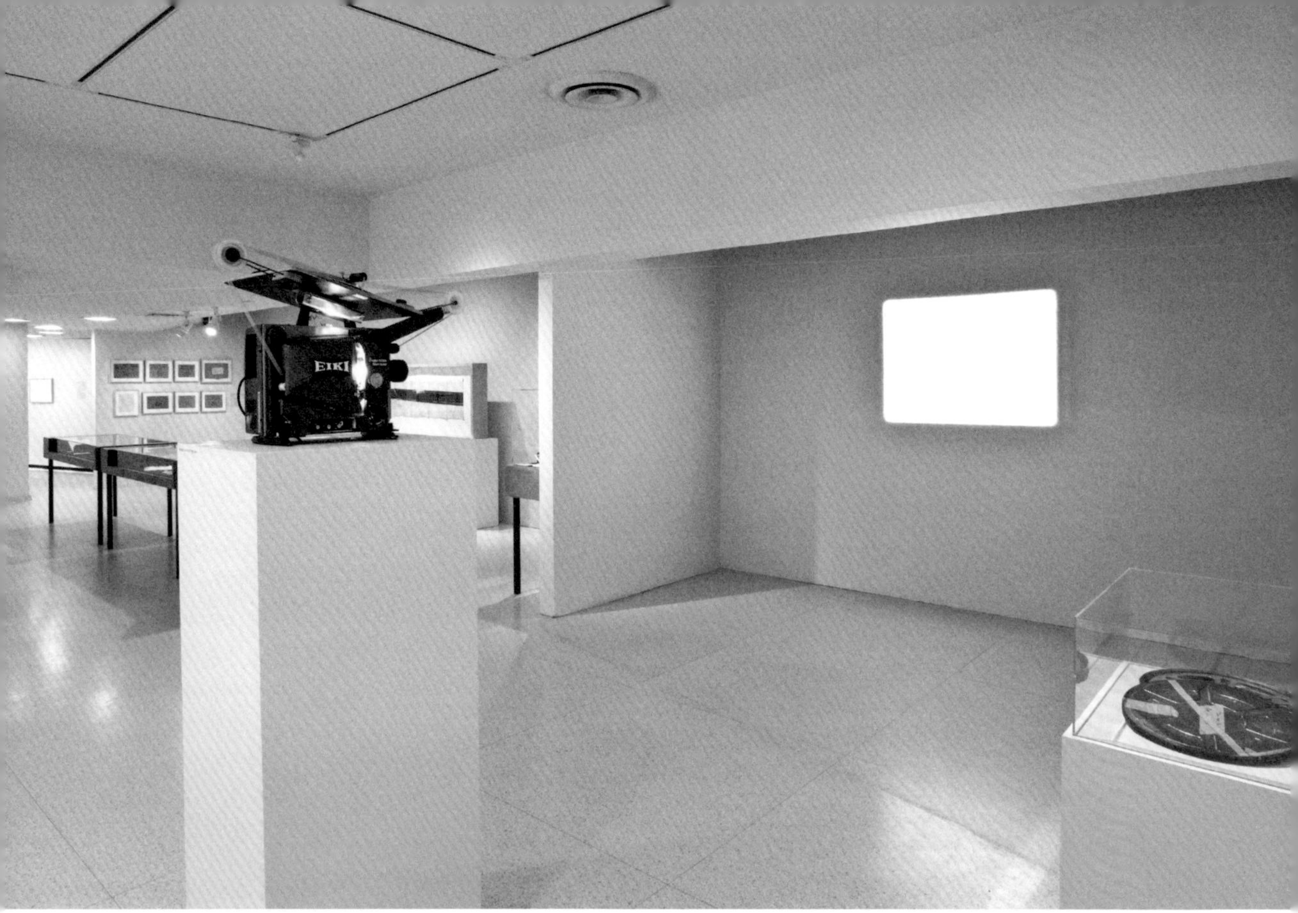

Fig. 10—*Zen for Film* installation in *The Third Mind: American Artists Contemplate Asia, 1860–1989*. Solomon R. Guggenheim Museum, New York. January 30–April 19, 2009. Photograph by David Heald. © SRGF, NY.

exposes the process of collecting traces and aspects of a cinematic event as an opportunity for an experience. In the Tate Liverpool variant of *Zen for Film*, the analogue film projection was replaced by a digital file beamed on the wall in the frozen condition of a hygienic, empty light rectangle. The wall caption revealed that this *Zen for Film* was a single-channel video, black-and-white, silent, eight minutes long (projected on a loop). A wall label also included the information "courtesy of the Electronic Art Intermix, EAI, New York." The EAI online database, in fact, holds a digital file of *Zen for Film* as part of *Fluxfilm Anthology* (fig. 11): "*Zen for Film*, Nam June Paik, 1962–64, 8 min, b&w, silent."[2] Both the EAI and the Tate labels hint at Paik's description of his film as a "clear film, accumulating in time, dust and scratches."[3] Whereas the EAI description, read in an online catalogue, might serve an informative purpose (we are more inclined to assume that the digital content of a website is different from the analogue character of the film), the Tate Liverpool installation claims a certain status for *Zen for Film* by projecting it as digital video. Apparently a curatorial decision, the digital projection inevitably signifies a mutation of the artist's initial intention, contained in the choice of a certain materiality of display. Clearly, the projection lacks the materiality of film, which is nowadays symptomatic of a number of exhibitions that include moving images, where DVD projections are substitutes for film (often in the case of Warhol). It is no less problematic to acknowledge that, as I pointed out earlier, *Zen for Film*, as a part of *Fluxfilm Anthology*, was probably manufactured by Maciunas for inclusion in a package of about forty films. Thus, the artwork's initial logic was already destabilized by "freezing" it into a singular film print. I will return to this aspect shortly.

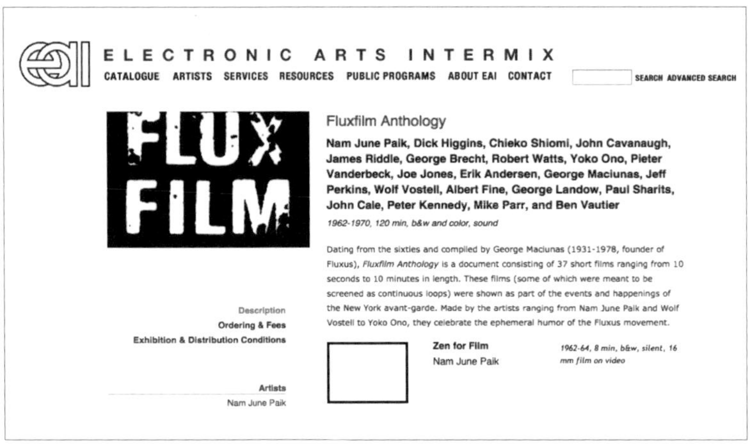

Fig. 11—Electronic Arts Intermix web page for George Maciunas, *Fluxfilm Anthology*, 1962–70, http://www.eai.org/title.htm?id=11976. Courtesy Electronic Arts Intermix (EAI), New York.

In the Tate variant (and in the digital version of *Fluxfilm Anthology*, distributed through various platforms) *Zen for Film* became an artwork with a finite relation to time. The film has been transferred through a digital file with a clear determination of duration—or a partial "documentation" of the work, as it were, a digital palimpsest of one of its screenings. The film leader and the infinite loop projecting itself endlessly have ceased to exist, lending a different element to the conceptual layers of the work. In this instance, *Zen for Film* lacks both the cinematic character of its analogue medium and the opportunity to experience a

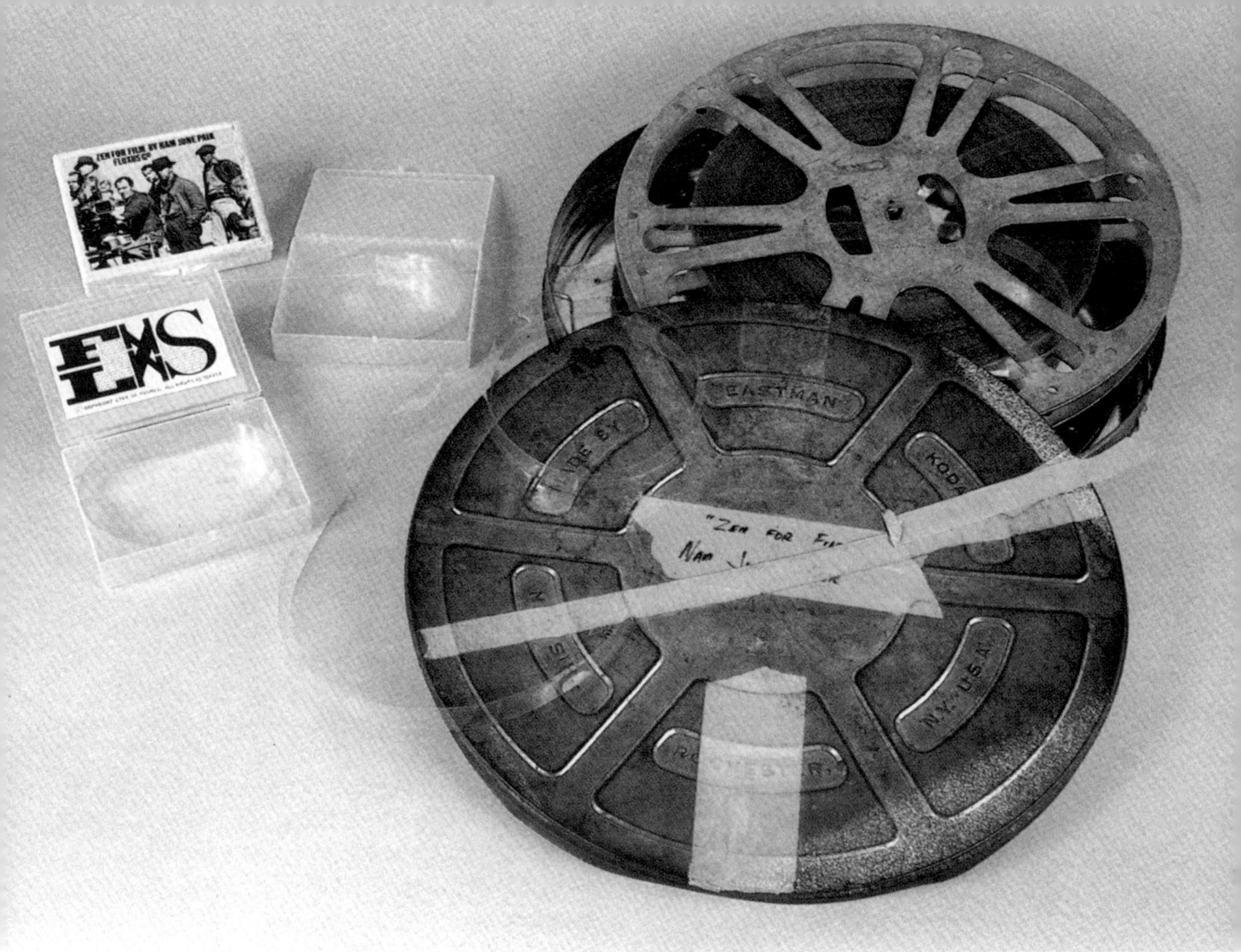

Fig. 12—Nam June Paik. *Zen for Film* as a filmic remnant from the 1960s (right) and three *Zen for Film* Fluxkit editions (left). Photograph by Brad Iverson. From *Fluxus Codex*. Detroit: Gilbert and Lila Silverman Fluxus Collection, 1988. © Nam June Paik Estate.

particular kind of duration. With its digitization, the process of collecting traces with each projection—as a witness of endless hours of analogue display intrinsic to the initial concept of *Zen for Film*—has been jettisoned, although the digital display in turn reveals traces other than just scratches, dust, and chance events, in other words, digital forms of decay. Additionally, the transformation into a digital video projection has a further implication: the screening becomes "silent," a radical reinterpretation of the initially rich sound experience dictated by the clattering mechanics of the projector. Whereas *Fluxfilm Anthology* appears to involve sound, Paik's film in this compilation is designated as silent. Either intentionally secured or intrinsic to the given technology, the noise of the apparatus may gain great importance and be considered as preservable in the form of a recording.[4] Clearly, stripping *Zen for Film* of the audible qualities of its mechanics is a radical move.

The film can for *Zen for Film*, encasing a blank film leader (fig. 12), is believed to be a remnant of film projections from the 1960s and is a part of the Gilbert and Lila Silverman Fluxus Collection at MoMA. Cage recalls that Paik invited his partner, the modern dancer and choreographer Merce Cunningham, to his studio on Canal Street to watch a "one-hour-long imageless film."[5] The film can, then, is a deactivated element of the earlier projection long-since decayed by time. As Jon Hendricks, Fluxus artist and curator of the Gilbert and Lila Silverman Fluxus Collection, reveals, the Silverman collection holds the only long film version of *Zen for Film*. According to Hendricks, it was played several times before being acquired for the Silverman collection. After the acquisition, when the work was loaned for external exhibitions, playing it was not allowed because of its brittle, fragile condition. The work was increasingly presented in a film can while a new film leader (a loop) was played on a film projector. Hendricks legitimizes this by claiming that *Zen for Film*, being an experience rather than an object, is about the reconstruction of an experience, and that using the old leader, which lies safely in the can, is unnecessary for this reconstruction.[6] Hendricks also recalls a VHS version of *Zen for Film* and regards its creation as a radical misinterpretation.[7] The video version presents itself as a sort of equivalent of the digital file extracted from *Fluxfilm Anthology*, despite their being tied to different technologies and media (the first, videotape; the second, film, most probably migrated to video and to an archival digital file—both versions a sort of frozen material of *Zen for Film*).

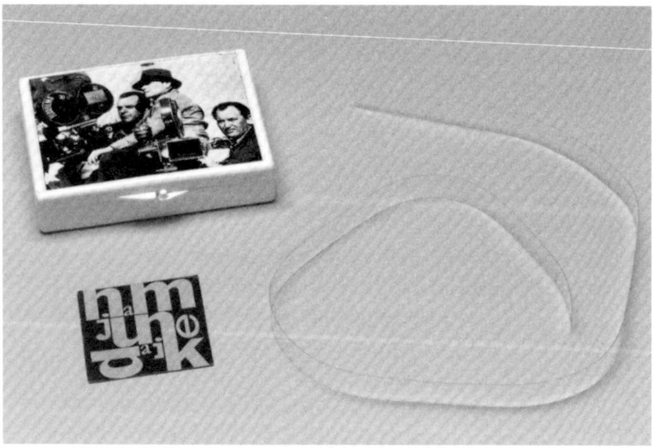

Fig. 13—Nam June Paik. *Zen for Film*, ca. 1965. Assembled and designed by George Maciunas. Plastic box with offset label, containing blank film loop and offset card. The Museum of Modern Art, The Gilbert and Lila Silverman Fluxus Collection Gift, 2627.2008.a-c. © The Museum of Modern Art / Licensed by SCALA / Art Resource, NY. © 2015 Nam June Paik Estate.

Lacking in these encounters, but included in the exhibition, is *Zen for Film* in the form of a Fluxus edition. These editions include a transparent or white box with—varying by version—one or multiple short strips of film leader (fig. 13). Was the Fluxus edition a replacement for the film run through the projector, or was it an object in its own right? I asked myself this up until October 2012, when I was able to hold the filmstrip in my hands.[8] The yellowed film was obviously too brittle and fragile to be projected.[9] Was it ever projected? What purpose, if any, would be served by projecting it?

So *what*, *where*, and *how* is *Zen for Film*? The answer to this and other questions can only be sought by looking more closely at the logic behind *Zen for Film* and by considering its emergence from a range of perspectives.

Notes

1—*The Third Mind* exhibition also involved a projection of the film, which I have chosen not to discuss here.
2—EAI online database, accessed November 10, 2014, http://www.eai.org/title.htm?id=11976. See also the section titled "The Film" in the introduction.
3—Ibid.; author's documentation of the Tate exhibition (personal files).
4—Bruce Nauman is known for his insistence on preserving the sonic experience of film projections that have been transferred to digital formats (for example, at the EAI). See also an interview with Nauman in Pip Laurenson, "Authenticity, Change and Loss in the Conservation of Time-Based Media Installations," *Tate Papers* 6 (2006), accessed December 12, 2011, www.tate.org.uk/download/file/fid/7401.
5—Cage, "Zum Werk von Nam June Paik," 22.
6—Jon Hendricks (consulting curator of the Silverman Fluxus Collection at MoMA), in discussion with the author, December 2010, May and December 2014.
7—The tape belongs to the Silverman Fluxus Collection, now at MoMA, and enjoys an ambiguous status somewhere between artifact and documentation. The inscription on the tape, "5.24.91," points to the date of its fabrication.
8—Erik Andersch Collection, Nam June Paik Art Center, Seoul.
9—The process of degradation of a film depends on its composition. Whereas polyester stock is rather stable and only embrittles when exposed to certain atmospheric conditions (ambient light and weather), in acetate stock, the triacetate deterioration includes a "vinegar syndrome" (the acetic acid affects the film base) and a color shift toward the red spectrum.

2nd Revision—

Zen, Nothingness, Boredom

Starting with nothing is a good way to get somewhere.
—Dick Higgins

At first sight, nothingness, emptiness, and visual stillness seem to constitute *Zen for Film*. These concepts are bound up, on the one hand, with the 1960s–70s avant-garde strategies of negation and, on the other, with Zen's ascetic withdrawal from the richness of visual representation. The idea of nothingness belongs to the core of Asian philosophy, notably Buddhism and Daoism, but it has also occupied Western philosophy, prominently in the philosophical projects of Martin Heidegger and Jean-Paul Sartre. In Western painting, voids and a certain visual austerity superseded styles marked by excess and abundance. In the 1960s, the Japanese aesthetic of stillness became increasingly attractive to Westerners, as did Zen, which disdains abundance in favor of simplicity.

The somewhat negative associations with death, absence, disappearance, and deficiency familiar in Western culture are viewed somewhat differently in the Eastern context. In the Daoist and Buddhist mindset nothingness becomes a fertile source inherent in everything that exists. The Heart Sutra, a popular Buddhist scripture, proclaims: "Form is emptiness, emptiness is form." By encouraging viewers to engage with the work, Paik deliberately asks them to empty their minds and allow an awareness of nothingness to arise. This process, if successful, may bring about another form of consciousness and sensitization in the beholder. "Art is everywhere; it's only seeing which stops now and then," maintained Cage.[1]

By enabling both an abandonment of preconceptions and the ability to perceive things as they manifest themselves in the "fullness of being," Zen practice seeks to achieve a profound unification with the world.[2] It is interesting, however, that Paik felt close to Zen aesthetics through the powerful influence of Cage rather than through his own cultural inheritance. Undoubtedly, Cage's spiritual dominance was unequivocal in Paik's works of the late 1950s and early 1960s. This relationship remained not without complications, as conveyed in one of Paik's statements: "I am an artist. . . . Because I am a friend of John Cage, people tend to see me as a Zen monk. . . . I'm not a follower of Zen but I react to Zen in the same way as I react to Johann Sebastian Bach."[3] Although Zen Buddhism originated in the sixth century in China and was only later developed in Korea and Japan, the kind of Zen that inspired Western artists, particularly in American artistic circles, has its roots in Japan.[4] Japanese scholar and writer Daisetz Teitaro Suzuki was deeply preoccupied with Zen and Shin Buddhism and played a crucial role in advancing Zen philosophy in the West.[5] Even though Paik's position in relation to Zen is ambiguous, Zen Buddhism certainly made its mark on his artistic practice. Suzuki's withdrawal from pictorial content—the seeing of Nothing as being the real, eternal seeing[6]—was probably the most effective of his teachings for Paik. In an interview with Justin Hoffman (Wiesbaden, May 22, 1989), Paik explained that aesthetic considerations dominated his attitude toward Eastern thought. He picked the title of another of his works, *Zen for TV* (1963), solely for aesthetic reasons: "The title is an artistic coincidence, you know. It is a beautiful title."[7] In the "Afterlude" to his 1963 Wuppertal exhibition, where, among other Zen works, *Zen for TV* premiered, Paik distances himself from Zen ideology entirely.[8]

Despite Paik's disavowal, *Zen for Film* shares a number of aspects with Zen compositions: among them, the description of the inherent nature of an aesthetic object by the simplest possible means; understanding the inner nature of an object—its "Buddha nature"—before emphasizing the essence (an artwork is already a work of natural art before the arrival of the artist on the scene); assigning minimal importance to the execution of the object because comprehension of the essence renders technique superfluous; and, also in line with Fluxus, experimentalism (reflected in using the simplest possible means, elevating everyday situations to art/events, and conjoining art with life). For *Zen for Film*—all one really needs is blank film leader and a projector. Paik delegates the labor to the projector itself, which produces the tangible traces of its own process. Appearing during the heyday of cinephilia and the beginnings of live electronic broadcast in the early 1960s, Paik's blank film evokes a lack of control that is only superficial. In a more profound direction, *Zen for Film* pushes the perceptual abilities of the spectator to the extreme. The work presents the

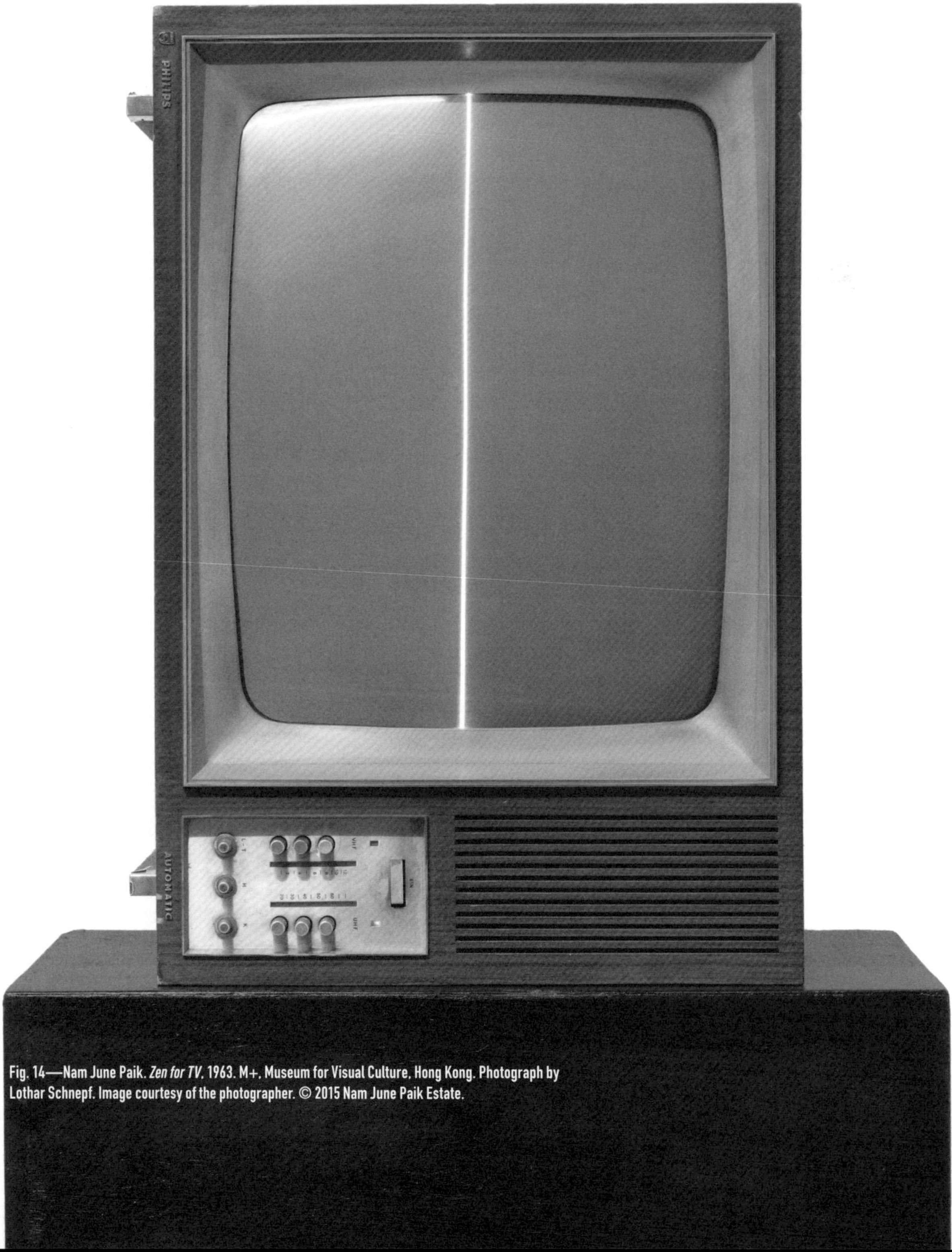

Fig. 14—Nam June Paik. *Zen for TV*, 1963. M+, Museum for Visual Culture, Hong Kong. Photograph by Lothar Schnepf. Image courtesy of the photographer. © 2015 Nam June Paik Estate.

extended dimension of a cinematic "timescape," an antispectacle proximate with but also far from whiteness, an epitome of nothingness. Are we watching a no-thing? Are we not watching some-thing?

Thus, *Zen for Film* can be seen as a part of Paik's series of works inspired by Zen philosophy, such as *Zen for TV* (1963; fig. 14), but also by *Zen for Head* (1962; fig. 15), *Zen for Wind* (1963), and *Zen for Nose* (1963). The incorporation of chance events connects *Zen for TV* with *Zen for Film*. During the preparation of *Exposition of Music*, where the work was first presented, a TV set broke—its image collapsed into a single line—and it was turned on its side. With its minimalist aesthetics and mystic aura, the line occurred as an electronic vertical Zenga (a Zen style of painting that uses quick, expressive brush strokes that follow intuition and immediacy).[9] Implementing the strategy of chance, in *Zen for Head* Paik obeys La Monte Young's instruction from *Composition 19 #10 (to Bob Morris)*: "Draw a straight line and follow it." Along the same lines, *Zen for Wind* employs *objets sonores*—"instruments" such as keys, tin cans, and wooden sandals hung from the ceiling, activated, just like *Zen for Nose*, by the viewer.[10]

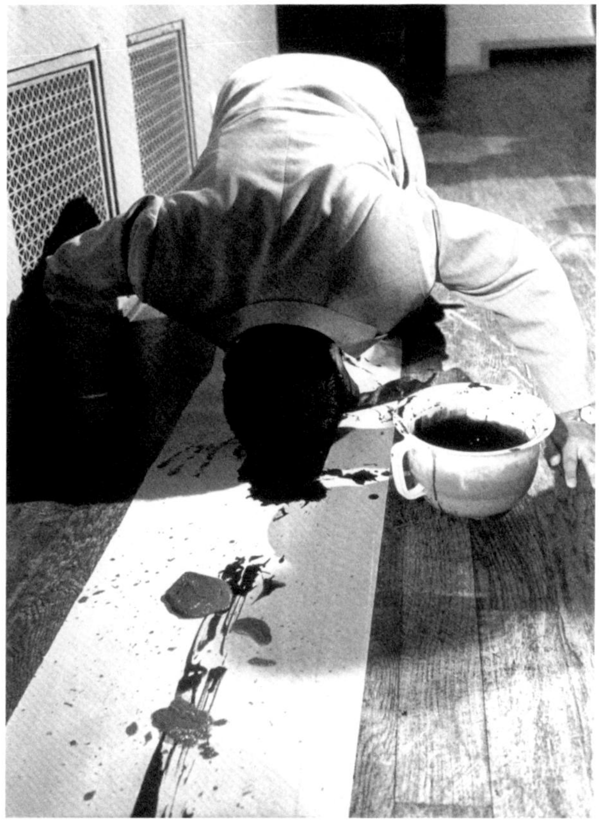

Fig. 15—Nam June Paik. *Zen for Head*, 1962. *Fluxus Festspiele neuster Musik*, Wiesbaden, September 1–23, 1962. Fluxus event in Wiesbaden, West Germany. Goettert / picture-alliance /dpa / AP Images.

Chance and contingency link Paik's work to Cage's method of composition. Related to the works of Zen artists, it involves the act of isolating the element of chance and providing random information based on procedures derived from *I Ching* (The Classic of Changes), an ancient Chinese book.[11] Following the motto "just let the sounds be themselves,"[12] Cage later began testing methods of indeterminate composition, creating fully or partially silent scores based on star maps. Cage's *4′33″* (1952), perhaps the most famous of his pieces (which I will discuss shortly), is an example; the piece shares the ideas of both Zen aesthetics and indeterminism with Paik's *Zen for Film*.

—

As I have suggested, nothingness, emptiness, and visual stillness, which constitute Paik's *Zen for Film*, are bound by the 1960s–70s avant-garde strategies of negation—or even refusal—of representation, facing, as it were, the increasing complexity of reality. With nothingness, so it seems, art reaches its zero point, as manifested five decades earlier by Kazimir Malevich, who painted his *White on White* (1918) and presented it along with suprematist canvases and other works during his first solo exhibition in Moscow.[13] László Moholy-Nagy's treatise *The New Vision: Fundamentals of Bauhaus Design, Painting, Sculpture, and Architecture* (1928) offers an interesting connection with *Zen for Film*'s cinematic nothingness. Moholy-Nagy discusses Malevich's *White on White*, interpreting it as a projection surface, a "plain white surface, which constituted an ideal plane for a kinetic light and shadow effect, which, originating in the surroundings, would fall upon it. In this way, Malevich's picture represents a miniature cinema screen."[14] Duchamp, too, seemed to reach this zero point when, in 1919, he turned against what he called "retinal art," art intended primarily for the eye, while presenting a pharmacy vial filled with Paris air (*50 cc of Paris Air*). This tendency toward invisible art was pushed further by Yves Klein's "monochrome voids," an exhibition of an empty gallery space in which the only object displayed was a case painted white at the Galerie Iris Clert in Paris (*Le Vide*, 1958), as well as his plans for *architecture de l'air*[15] and air sculptures created together with Jean Tinguely (1958).

The reduction of the representation sphere or cinematic vision can also be seen as a response to modernism's "rhetoric of iconoclasm."[16] Aimed at abandoning any signs and symbols involved in traditional imagery, this rhetoric was materialized in the nonfigurative gestural abstraction of the postwar era. Modern art had entered a "period of latency" in which, as Lucio Fontana argues in his 1946 manifesto, "painted canvas and standing plaster figures no longer have any reason to exist."[17] Although Paik must have experienced postwar trauma during his years in Japan and Germany after fleeing the Korean War, it would be far-fetched to search for the conditions that rendered his filmic work empty in the aftermath of the Second World War and Hiroshima—and the impossibility of making art after the apparent breakdown of liberal humanism.[18]

How does *Zen for Film*, then, reflect the aesthetic tendencies of its time? The American critic Clement Greenberg admonished artists to expel any iconography and narrativity in painting by using the painted surface as an end in itself.[19] Paik's *Zen for Film* seems to perform this expulsion in relation to film rather than a painted surface. Implementing a clear filmstrip as an end in itself abandons representation (signs and symbols) for the purity of the visible; the process of projection exposes the material quality and mechanical structure of the medium. To use the rhetoric of iconoclasm, *Zen for Film*'s sheer materiality, while destroying pictorial representation, "exhausts itself in the visual sensation it produces."[20] As art and image theorist Hans Belting puts it in relation to the avant-garde's omnipotence of gesture, "seeing is purged [of] seeing images."[21]

The idea of the abandonment of representation extends to two of Paik's other artworks presented in Wuppertal—*Point of Light* (1963), an electronic image reduced to a point in the center of the screen (fig. 16), and *Rembrandt Automatic* (1963), a TV turned with the screen facing the floor (fig. 17). These artworks demonstrate Paik's interest in expressing more with less by means of a surprising minimization of visual content. They also evoke Kaprow's idea of the direct implementation of objects in the making of art, so that the desire for immediacy replaces the wish to represent. "Objects of every sort are materials for the new art," according to Kaprow. "Paint, chairs, food, electric and neon lights, smoke, water, old socks, a dog, movies, a thousand other things."[22] Although Kaprow's motivation was inspired by Jackson Pollock's transition from painting to the act of its making, *Zen for Film* seems to relate to the idea of direct art making in a double sense: it is a simple projection of a blank film, translated into art—in a Duchampian sense—by Paik's act of designating it as such,[23] and it is (and is in) a process of constant becoming through gathering traces, smudges, and dust.

—

Zen for Film stands clearly in opposition to Paik's later abundance of visual noise and collages of film sequences, eclectic passages from earlier videos, and recycled film stills. Although, as I have suggested, the act of projecting an empty film may have nihilist and perhaps also iconoclastic connotations (evocative of Fluxus's anti-art ideology), placed on the continuum of Paik's artistic development the film may also represent a certain quieting after his action and music performances, which entailed destructive acts as a means of rebellion against ruling conventions in music.[24] Especially during performances in Germany in the early 1960s, Paik effectively used an element of shock as a means of affecting and altering the viewer's self-perception.[25] One notorious example is the slaughtered head of a bull presented at the entrance to his Parnass exhibition in Wuppertal, which, according to Paik, "made more sensation than 13 TV sets."[26] One might speculate that the element of shock employed in *Zen for Film* has different qualities: divorcing himself from the shock generated by the horror of the brutal, unexpected experience, Paik channels the shock to the unexpectedly reduced visual proposition—to apparent stillness, nothingness, oblivion. In contrast to galleries crowded by objects and to the pace of information in the digital age, *Zen for Film* remains as intriguing today as it did at the moment of its creation.

And yet Paik's film is clearly not only about whiteness, nothingness, and emptiness, but also about the impossibility of the complete reduction of the visual. In its materiality, *Zen for Film* pays homage to Cage's seminal *4′33″*, in which the interpreters are instructed not to play their instruments for the entire duration

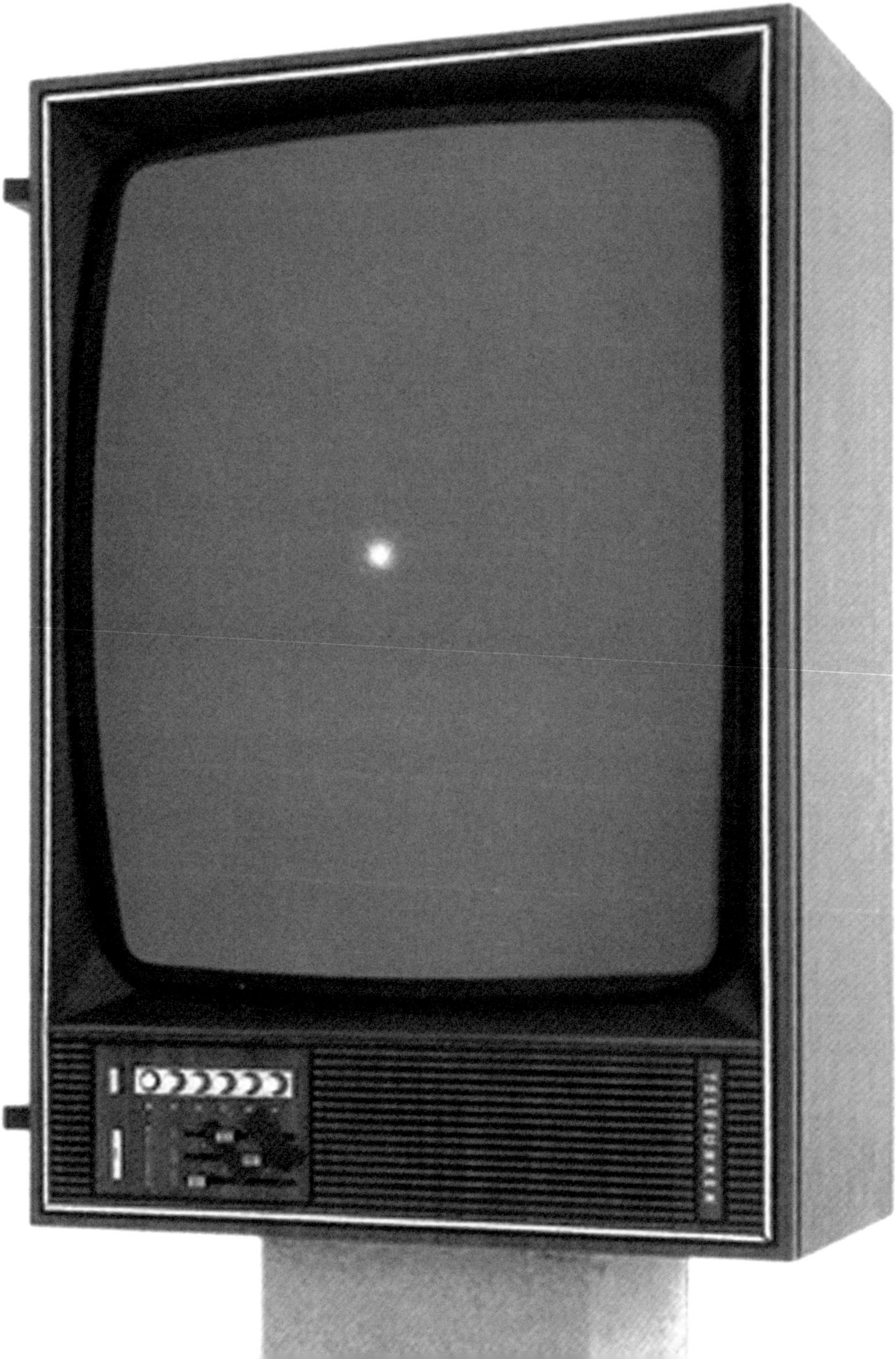

Fig. 16—Nam June Paik. *Point of Light (Zen for TV)*, 1963/91. Neue Nationalgalerie, Berlin. © Nam June Paik Estate.

of the piece's three movements, allowing the ambient sounds of the environment to do the work (fig. 18).[27] In addition to the act of removing the interpreter's active involvement (in the sense of "playing music")—when a piano is used, the interpreter opens and closes the lid to mark the beginning and end of each movement—Cage's work introduces the laws of chance, questioning the role of the composer and imposing agency on the listener. The sheer impossibility of silence in *4′33″* resonates in Paik's blank film in the impossibility of visual nothingness; it is as impossible to experience pure silence as it is to experience complete visual nothingness. Because the film is essentially about transparency, a clear frame proves the impossibility of an empty image. In his essay "Indeterminacy" (1973), Cage describes a Chinese poetry contest in which the mind is compared to a mirror: "The mind is like a mirror, it collects dust. The problem is to remove the dust." This is continued in another poem that questions: "Where is the mirror and where is the dust?" It is striking that, although Paik underlined his close connection to the composer, Cage himself stresses that it is *Zen for Film* that united and, simultaneously, separated Paik and himself. According to Cage, *Zen for Film* is Paik's own *4′33″*, yet Paik's stillness is produced in an image, whereas Cage's stillness comes from tone.[28]

—

Zen for Film can be viewed not only as an example of Zen-like withdrawal from imagery but also as a tribute to Robert Rauschenberg's *White Painting* (1951), which chronologically preceded Cage's most prominent romance with silence (fig. 19).[29] "Offhand, you might say that all three actions are the same. But they are quite different," stated Cage in reference to Rauschenberg's work, Paik's, and his own. "Nam June Paik's film has no images on it; the

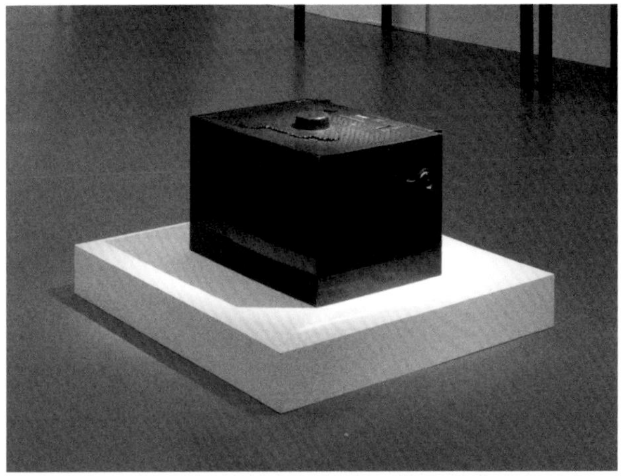

Fig. 17—Nam June Paik. *Rembrandt Automatic* installation in *Nam June Paik: Video Artist, Performance Artist, Composer and Visionary*. Tate Liverpool, December 17, 2010–March 13, 2011. © Tate, London 2015.

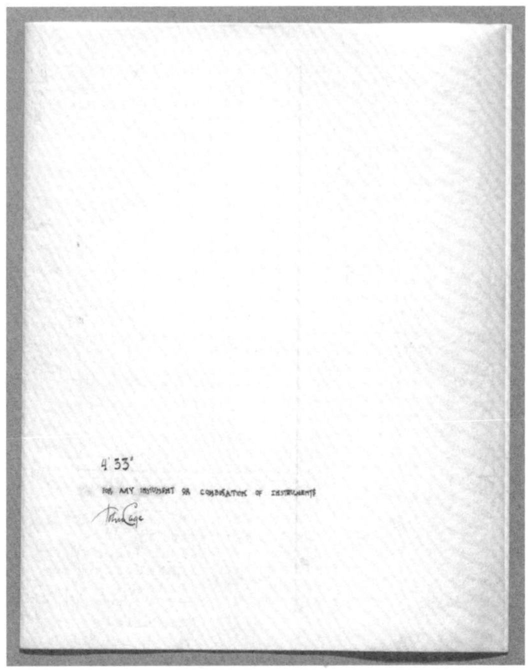

Fig. 18—John Cage. *4′33″ (In Proportional Notation)*, 1952/1953. Ink on paper. © The Museum of Modern Art / Licensed by SCALA / Art Resource, NY. The Museum of Modern Art, Acquired through the generosity of Henry Kravis in honor of Marie-Josée Kravis, 1636.2012. © 1960 by Henmar Press Inc. Used by permission of C. F. Peters Corporation.

room is darkened, the film is projected, and what you see is the dust that has collected on the film. I think that's somewhat similar to the case of the Rauschenberg painting, though the focus is more intense."[30] Indeed, in Moore's photograph taken during the New Cinema Festival I, Paik's silhouette remains captured as a shadow on the screen of the projection of *Zen for Film*, resembling Rauschenberg's screens reflecting the slightest of ambient conditions in fleeting impressions.[31] This association returns us to Malevich's *White on White*, which Moholy-Nagy compared to a projection surface. The "concerted action" that Cage directed at Black Mountain College in 1952 included Rauschenberg's paintings hung "in different angles, a canopy of pictures above the audience," serving as screens for the projection of films and abstract slides.[32]

Cage—Rauschenberg's friend and close collaborator—often admitted that he was inspired by Rauschenberg's eccentricity. In *Silence* (1973), Cage notes that the panels of *White Painting* "were airports of the lights, shadows, and particles," "mirrors of the air" that provide a substrate for observing change and infinite visual possibilities.[33] Although *White Painting* can be seen as naturally "Zen," it also coincides with Rauschenberg's idea of his canvas as a "hypersensitive" picture plane.[34] His belief that "a canvas is never empty" is mirrored in Cage's approach to silence, and, subsequently, Paik's seemingly empty projection.[35] Cage maintains that when he first encountered Rauschenberg's *White Painting* series, he was already thinking about a composition entailing only silence, but the paintings triggered him to "immediately respond to them," leading to the creation of *4′33″*.[36] "Silence, like music, is non-existent," Cage contends. "There are always sounds."[37] Therefore, Rauschenberg's pictorial, Cage's musical, and Paik's filmic silence are devoid of otherworldliness and reluctance to communicate.[38] Rather, their renunciation of conventional modes of communication through artistic means sharpens the perceptual attention of the spectators; nevertheless, the three artworks—*4′33″*, *White Painting*, and *Zen for Film*—all manifest fundamental differences concerning vision (Rauschenberg), sound (Cage), and time (Paik).

—

Despite the array of intriguing conceptual and historical connections, watching *Zen for Film* might also elicit a state of boredom. Conventionally, the term "boredom" carries negative connotations; however, in the context of Fluxus, as Dick Higgins puts it, boredom ceases to be something to be avoided and comes to be deliberately employed by artists.[39] Paik claims that "boredom itself is far from being a negative quality. In Asia, it is rather a sign of nobility."[40] In her essay "Boredom and Oblivion," Ina Blom argues that as the result of boredom, "the work will disappear into the surroundings, and the spectator will disappear into the work."[41]

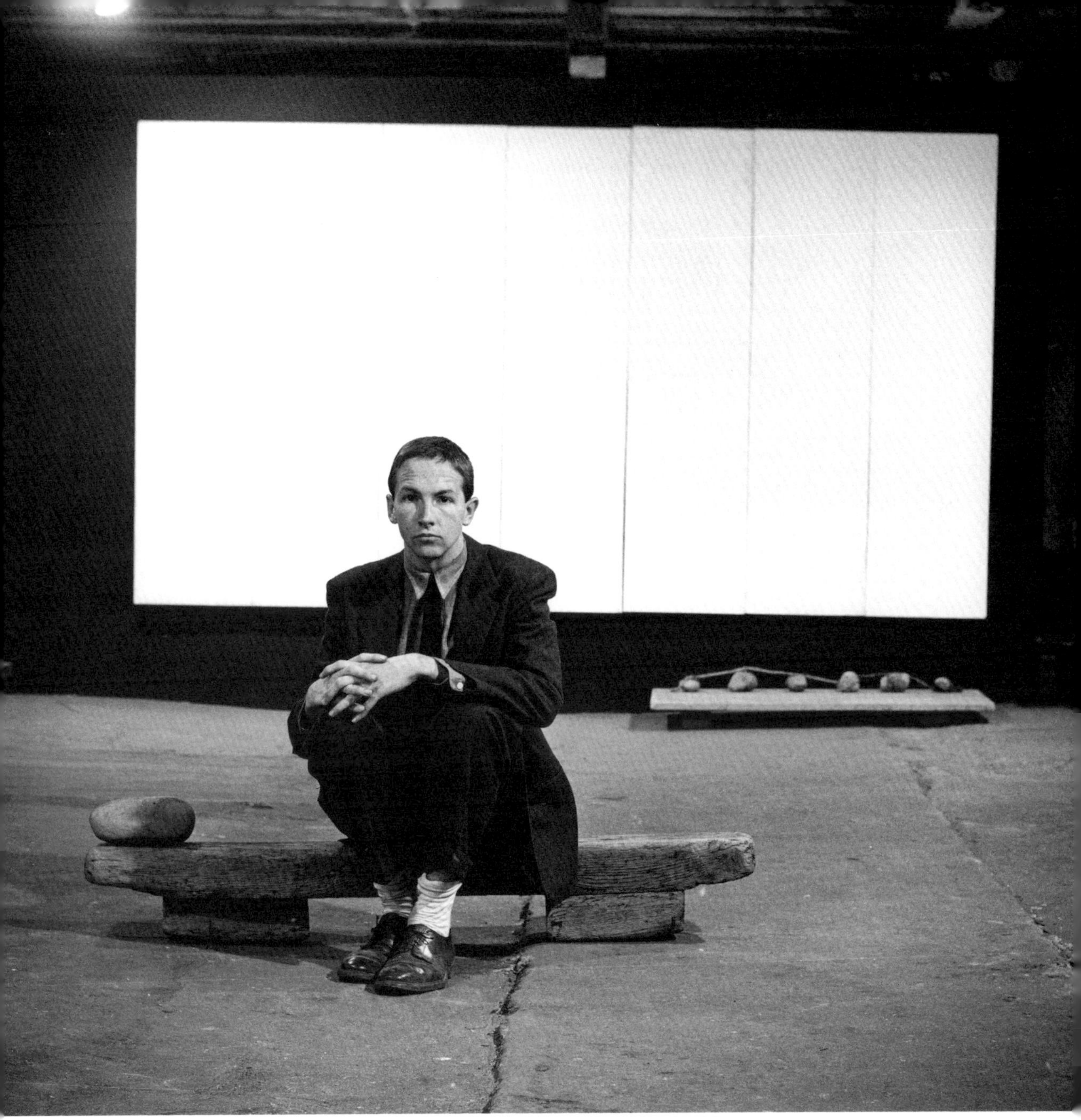

Fig. 19—Robert Rauschenberg at *Robert Rauschenberg: Paintings and Sculpture*, Stable Gallery, New York, 1953. Works shown are *White Painting* [seven panel] (1951) and two untitled *Elemental Sculptures* (both 1953). Photograph by Allan Grant / The LIFE Picture Collection / Getty Images.

The immersion of the subject in the environment will result in the condition of "oblivion or unknowing," leading eventually to the experience of the void described by Paik in relation to Cage's concerts.[42]

An extended viewing of *Zen for Film* can facilitate a profound spatiotemporal experience not only of the apparatus but also of our own existence through a direct experience of time. Heidegger, who introduced perhaps the most extensive philosophical treatment of boredom, describes one form of boredom using the example of waiting for a train at a provincial station.[43] If we believe Heidegger, dealing with raw time within the vacuum created by the absence of the conventional noise of modern life—telephones, newspapers, the Internet, and other people—can evoke a feeling of discomfort. When we have no other occupation that might distract us, then time pushes down on us, making us aware of our surroundings and of ourselves, our existence.[44]

Paik seems to have been preoccupied with the boredom *of*, and *in*, his works. *Exposition of Music* aimed to reach a dimension of depth that is difficult to grasp physically. As a liminal aesthetic experience—and as exemplified by *Zen for Film*—Paik believed in boredom's boundary-dissolving capacity, which liberated it from the dichotomy between the ugly and the beautiful:

> try it
> initially, it might (probably) be interesting for you—
> then it will become boring—
> don't give up! ["aushalten!"]
> then it might (probably) become interesting again—
> then boring again—
> don't give up!
> then it might (probably) become interesting again—
> then boring again—
> don't give up![45]

Elsewhere, he writes: "Anyway, if you see my TV, please, see it more than 30 minutes."[46]

Notes

1—Lewallen, "Cage and the Structure of Chance," 227.
2—See Doris, "Zen Vaudeville," 94.
3—Paik in an interview with Otto Hahn (1992), quoted in Rhee, "Reconstructing the Korean Body," 48.
4—For a discussion of Zen, its alleged split between Northern and Southern schools, and its impact on Fluxus, see Friedman, "Introduction," x.

5—For Suzuki, Zen, because of its ephemeral nature, was almost impossible to characterize. He claimed that even the slightest attempt to catch a glimpse of it causes it to disappear. It is also important to note that Suzuki was not the sole generator of interest in Zen in Western artistic circles. In the 1950s, books on haiku, Zen painting, calligraphy, and martial arts were already available. See Westgeest, *Zen in the Fifties*, 11, 54.

6—See Zschocke, *Der irritierte Blick*, 313.

7—Paik and Hoffman, "Interview in a Station Restaurant," 84.

8—Paik, "Afterlude to the Exposition of Experimental Television."

9—See Pollard and Stevens, *Zen Mind Zen Brush*; Lutz, *Mystik*.

10—See Landy and Graevenitz, "I Make Technology Ridiculous," 89–90.

11—See Kacunko, *Closed Circuit Videoinstallationen*, 170.

12—Cage, *Silence*, 70.

13—See Anna Dezeuze, "The Void," *Nothing Works* (Tate blog), January 1, 2011, http://www.tate.org.uk/context-comment/articles/nothing-works.

14—Moholy-Nagy, quoted in Branden, *Random Order*, 36.

15—See Rugoff, *Invisible*, 5.

16—W. J. T. Mitchell, quoted in Belting, "Beyond Iconoclasm," 390.

17—See Fontana, "Manifesto Blanco (1946)," 47.

18— See Selz and Stiles, "Gestural Abstraction," in *Theories and Documents of Contemporary Art*, 13 (referring to German philosopher Theodor Adorno's well-known dictum, "To write poetry after Auschwitz is barbaric").

19—Greenberg, "Towards a Newer Laocoön."

20—John O'Brian, quoted in Belting, "Beyond Iconoclasm," 391.

21—Ibid.

22—Kaprow, "The Legacy of Jackson Pollock," 7–9.

23—Maciunas places *Zen for Film* under the category "readymades & found film." Maciunas, "Some Comments on 'Structural Film' by P. Adams Sitney," 349.

24—Smashing a violin on a table in a darkened space, smashing eggs, overturning a piano, cutting off Cage's tie, and shredding his clothes belonged to Paik's repertoire. See Meigh-Andrews, *A History of Video Art*, 13; Herzogenrath, "When the Future Was Now."

25—See Brill, *Shock and the Senseless in Dada and Fluxus*, 147.

26—Paik, "Afterlude."

27—The three tacets of *4′33″* indicate silence on the part of the performer. During the first performance in Woodstock, New York, on August 29, 1952, the young American pianist David Tudor, himself a composer of experimental music, divided the piece into three sections marked by the closing and opening of the piano's lid in intervals of 33″, 2′40″, and 1′20″. See also Herman Asselberghs, "Beyond the Appearance of Imagelessness: Preliminary Notes on Zen for Film's Enchanted Materialism," *Afterall* (Autumn/Winter 2009), accessed December 22, 2014, http://www.afterall.org/journal/issue.22/beyond.the.appearance.of.imagelessness.preliminary.notes.on.zen.for.films.enchanted.materialism.

28—See Cage, "Zum Werk von Nam June Paik," 22.

29—*White Painting*—created using the simple means of a roller and latex house paint—became open to reiterations as a piece based on instructions offering the possibility of remaking it "all white" on two, three, four, five, and seven panels. For the instructions, see Bois et al., *The Anarchy of Silence*, 178.

30—Cage on Nam June Paik in exhibition catalogue, Galeria Bonino, New York, 1971, quoted in Herzogenrath, *Nam June Paik Fluxus/Video*, 150.

31—The image in the photograph has led Christopher Eamon to interpret *Zen for Film* as a film about Paik's movements within the frame. He also claims that the performer is necessary to complete the work, associating Paik's film with Robert Whiteman's *Prune Flat* (1965) and Guy Debord's *Hurlements en faveur de Sade* (Howls in favor of Sade, 1952). Eamon, "An Art of Temporality," 66–85.

32—See Belting, "Beyond Iconoclasm," 391.

33—Cage, "On Robert Rauschenberg, Artist, and His Work," *Metro* 2 (May 1961): 43, 50; reprinted in Cage, *Silence*.

34—See Tomkins, *The Bride and the Bachelors*, 203.

35—Joseph, *Random Order,* 21. Although Rauschenberg did not confirm his attachment to Zen, Cage stated: "I spent years studying and trying to understand Zen. You, you have done nothing of the sort, you are just naturally Zen." Bérénice Bailly, "'J'aime le mouvement de la main,'" *Le Monde,* August 9, 2005, accessed January 4, 2015, http://www.lemonde.fr/culture/article/2005/08/09/robert-rauschenberg-j-aime-le-mouvement-de-la-main_678772_3246.html.

36—SFMOMA, "Robert Rauschenberg's *White Painting,*" John Cage and Robert Rauschenberg in the audio guide "The Art of Participation: 1950 to Now," accessed June 14, 2012, http://www.sfmoma.org/explore/multimedia/audio/aop_tour_404.

37—Cage, *Silence*, 152.

38—For the notion of silence as a refusal to communicate, see Sontag, "Aesthetics of Silence," 3–34.

39—Dick Higgins, "Boredom and Danger," *Something Else Newsletter* (December 1968; written in 1966), quoted in Blom, "Boredom and Oblivion," 63.

40—Paik, *Du cheval à Christo et autres écrits*, 198 (author's translation).

41—Blom, "Boredom and Oblivion," 66.

42—See Brill, *Shock and the Senseless*, 147.

43—Exploring the temporality of human existence and its relation to the meaning of existence, Heidegger's project includes three varieties of boredom: "becoming bored by something," "being bored with something," and "profound boredom." Heidegger, *The Fundamental Concepts of Metaphysics,* chs. 1–2. For the concept of boredom, see also Osborne, "The Dreambird of Experience."

44—Thinking about the awareness of existence though experiencing a vacuum is central to the philosophy of Jean-Paul Sartre.

45—Paik, "Beiblatt zur Einladung," n.p. Paik's statement follows the experience of the irrational koan, the repeated experience of which is purported to bring enlightenment. It also seems to follow Cage's earlier assertion regarding Zen: "In Zen they say, if something is boring after 2 minutes try it for 4. If still boring, try it for 8, 16, 32, and so on. Eventually one discovers that it's not boring at all but very interesting." Quoted in Westgeest, *Zen in the Fifties*, 80.

46—Paik, "Afterlude."

3rd Revision—

Time, Finitude, Transparency

At any rate, one must stress that this is neither painting nor sculpture, but a "temporal art."
—Nam June Paik

The relation between boredom and time is established within a prolonged temporal passing. For the spectator, time in *Zen for Film* happens somewhere in the realm of a hardly bearable experience of duration, demanding of the spectator the highest effort of endurance and meditative calmness. Yet there is another aspect of time involved in *Zen for Film*—the time of the filmic medium and its apparatus.

The time of *Zen for Film* is, first of all, time processed by a machine[1]—the projector—present in the movement of a filmstrip through its mechanism in a sequence of discrete images. In the process, it should become tangible, cinematic time, imprinted in instances of presents-that-have-been but simultaneously are-not-yet. Yet there is something peculiar about this temporal relationship; it conveys a skewed message. The film leader is empty, the frames—the time frames—nonexistent. Paik's blank filmstrip is not, as has often been asserted, an unexposed film. Rather, it is a clear film leader, conveying no message, no spatial intervals, and no temporal record in a cinematic sense.[2] Nothing has been stopped and turned into a frozen snapshot. The film subverts Henri Bergson's critique of cinema, in which he argues that the cinematograph (the combination camera-projector introduced in the late nineteenth century) substitutes frozen instances, frame by frame, for the fluidity of real motion and ceaseless, durational flux.[3] In *Zen for Film* there are no instances recorded, no photograms, or any kind of pictorial presence—motion exists only in the machine's pulling the transparent leader through its spools. The blinking illumination of the projector offers only a trace of traditional cinematic rhythm. Because there are no stoppages, no time frames and singular instances, *Zen for Film* becomes a subtle means of representing duration cinematically. In these terms, Paik allegorizes the temporal continuum in the filmic medium and provides the ultimate exemplification of Gilles Deleuze's conception of cinematic continuity.[4] Paradoxically, the noncontent of the film is also, and even more so, proof of the impossibility of representing pure duration. *Zen for Film*, then, does not embalm time as a photograph or filmic photogram by becoming an index or a record of a fraction of time. But what does it mean that Paik's film has no relation to any recorded image, no reference carried within itself? The answer to this question is crucial for understanding *Zen for Film* and the kind of temporality with which it confronts us.

In "The Ontology of the Photographic Image" (1945, English translation 1967), French film critic and theorist André Bazin identifies the origins of art in the human drive to overcome death and defines photography as a successful preserving gesture against the destructive influences of the flow of time.[5] A recurring motif in Roland Barthes's *Camera Lucida* (1980) is the presence of death, inscribed on life by photography—a click that separates the "initial pose from the final print"—corresponding to "a symbolic Death, outside of religion, outside of ritual."[6] The theme of death is taken on by Laura Mulvey, who, in her book *Death 24x a Second* (2006), adds new ways of conceptualizing the relation of film to time. Following Godard's conviction that a photograph freezes reality in its transition from animate to inanimate, from life to death, and that a film reverses the process by reanimating the static frames, Mulvey proposes to define the cinema as "death 24 times a second."[7] If a frame is a static image and, of necessity, characterized by a deathly aspect, Paik's blank film escapes from this stasis into the realm of nonrepresentation, distancing itself from the 1960s flicker film and its relation to stillness and movement, frame and the projector.[8] Because there is no static frame, no image as a photogram whatsoever, the actuality of *Zen for Film* is always sustained.[9] So Paik's film also transcends the cinematic death drive, the 24-times-a-second moments of frozen temporality, successful in circumventing the material condition of the filmic medium through the cinematic performance.

This is not to say, however, that Paik's work is unrelated to finitude as distinct from the cinematic death, which will, in effect, coincide with the trace, the dust and streaks on the film. *Zen for Film* does not, however, manage to escape another aspect of temporality, which crystallizes gradually in the evidence of the mechanical impact of its running time—the intervals of projection. Time persistently imprints its traces on the sensitive surface of the celluloid. Time marks the cyclical intervals of the projection, running in an endless, apparently seamless loop. This feature distinguishes analogue from digital versions of *Zen for Film*. The accumulation of analogue traces on the film leads to the obliteration of its content—or rather, the trace itself, the index of obliteration, becomes its visual content. What does it mean to have all these traces on the film, in an ever-condensing accumulation? Is time—the time of the machine—being not only inscribed on its surface but also compressed and, in a way, concentrated? A trace left by a person—a line on paper, for instance—has the ability to transport an object to another realm of existence. In analogue film, this role is taken over by a machine. *Zen for Film* clearly exemplifies the mechanical inscription of time: the imprint of the mechanical activity of the apparatus on the transparent film leader raises it to another realm. The exchangeability of the filmstrip, by opening up new possibilities of repeated time inscription, also suggests another form of circumventing the death drive. A new period of "usage" is initiated with every exchange of the film leader. A loop, however, succumbs to the trace faster than a "linear" version, a film played from a spool. From the point of view of the decision maker, the moment for replacing the film is dictated by its condition. Is there a moment when the film is sufficiently "used," ready to be replaced? When does the time imprint stop? When is it "completed"?

This accumulation of traces on the transparent filmstrip in *Zen for Film* takes us to the relationship between the imprint of time and the transparency of the film. The visible relationship between transparency and opacity is engaging insofar as transparency is commonly assigned a higher value than opacity. Transparency is relative, however, and may only be assessed in terms of a state of lesser or greater transparency. As time imprints its trace, the film leader gradually loses transparency, until it ultimately becomes opaque. Paik's filmic endeavor may, in fact, represent a critique of transparency. Transparency depends on avoiding alteration and preventing change in response to the flux of time. It enables undistorted seeing. Transparent works are timeless; thus, the imprint of time, in whatever form it might take, clearly complicates them. As Paik's film renders the transparent surface opaque, he also reveals the reality of the medium. Alteration, the loss of transparency, and decay may themselves become highly aesthetic experiences, as demonstrated in Bill Morrison's film *Decasia* (2002), which was created using found, archival nitrate stock. The film sets the beauty of decay against the deadly effects of time.[10] Paik's sidestep in the evolution of image culture—the maximum reduction of visual content in *Zen for Film* and its conceptual erasure of pictorial strata—recalls Robert Rauschenberg's *Erased de Kooning Drawing* of 1953, in which the unmaking of one work becomes simultaneously the creation of another by producing the trace of the removal of the trace.[11] The unmaking would signify the refusal of the narrative and the creation of an added (rather than reduced) value through the accumulation of the traces of time and decay. *Zen for Film* allows for a different kind of contemplation of decay, creating a remarkable form of aesthetic encounter.[12] The imprint of time in Paik's *Zen for Film* has a positive value that inverts the relationship between transparency, which enables seeing, and the loss of transparency, which imbues what is being seen (or what is becoming less visible and more opaque) with another quality. And rather than in an instant, this new dimension of seeing reveals itself in time, in duration.

Notes

1—For a temporal regime of media different from historical, anthropocentric time, see Ernst, "Media Archaeology," 250.

2—These types of carrier were implemented to color an existing film by tinting the desired areas on the clear leader and superimposing it on the film proper. The artist Jud Yalkut (1938–2013), in discussion with the author, June 2012.

3—Henri Bergson's view stems from his having written when cinema was in its infancy. See Deleuze, *Cinema 1*, 1–2.

4—In *Cinema 1* and *Cinema 2*, a profound analysis of the moving image in the last century, Deleuze criticizes Bergson for focusing on the intermittent mechanics of the apparatus rather than on the perceptual continuity of the moving image. The continuity, according to Deleuze, derives from the spectator's ability to perceive the intermediate image as a continuum and, simultaneously, the impossibility of seeing individual photograms. Deleuze, *Cinema 1*, 1–3.

5—Bazin, "The Ontology of the Photographic Image," 9–16. Photography's preserving gesture against the flow of time is evident, for instance, in the deathbed photograph's replacing the earlier death mask. See Mulvey, *Death 24x a Second*, 59.

6—Barthes, *Camera Lucida*, 92.

7—Mulvey, *Death 24x a Second,* 15. Mulvey's title stems from Jean-Luc Godard's assertion that cinema is "truth 24 times a second."

8—Tony Conrad's experimental film *The Flicker* (1965, 28 min.) is an example of the genre. Both *The Flicker* and *Zen for Film* share a strong relation to the projection apparatus.

9—The lack of photograms in Paik's film also contests the essentialism of Barthes's "The Third Meaning," in which Barthes locates the essence of cinema in film stills. Barthes, "The Third Meaning," 52–68.

10—In a different way from Paik's clear filmstrip, the decaying and decayed *Decasia* addresses the very process of change in altered archival film footage, evoking simultaneously positive (beauty of decay) and negative (deadly effects of time) connotations. *Decasia* is accompanied by a recording of a symphony by Michael Gordon.

11—In Rauschenberg's *Erased de Kooning*, the vandalism of obliterating de Kooning's drawing is set against the value of the composition that resulted. The negation becomes a creation and a conservation gesture of sorts.

12—The material (physical and chemical) change of the leader will occur independently of the imprinting of new traces. The imprinting process, as it overtakes the pace of material-specific decay, determines whether the film is in operable condition.

4th Revision—

Linearity, Circularity, Editions

Zen for Film's multiplicity of existence (portrayed in revision 1) might be both a blessing and a curse, especially when it comes to an attempt to establish a certain historical order or genealogy for the emergence of its many variants. Similarly, there may be more questions than answers to the tentatively set dates for when Paik's film and its editions emerged, a situation that requires some exploration.

To a great extent, a genealogy can be deduced from Hendricks's copious records of Fluxus editions in the Silverman collection. From his anthology of Fluxus events assembled in *Fluxus Etc. / Addenda II*, we learn that *Zen for Film* and another of Paik's works, tentatively titled "Fluxus Contest for Piano?," were featured together as part of *Concert No. 5* (April 25), which took place during the *Twelve Fully Guaranteed Fluxus Concerts* festival (March–May 1964) at the Fluxhall in New York.[1] In turn, *Concert No. 8* (May 8, 1964) featured *Zen for Film* as an individual event. Additionally, *Fluxus Etc.* includes another mention of Paik's films—screened during *Festum Fluxorum: Poésie, Musique et Antimusique Événementielle et Concrète* at the American Center for Students and Artists in Paris on December 6, 1962—that may have involved a screening of *Zen for Film*.[2]

The uncertain beginnings of *Zen for Film* are complicated even more by the emergence of its Fluxus edition, which Maciunas produced sometime between 1964 and 1965. In *Fluxus Codex*, Hendricks notes that "*Zen for Film* exists in two distinct Fluxus versions: a small boxed edition, usually with the Maciunas-designed label (Silverman No. 355), and a long 16mm version suitable for theater showings (Silverman No. 354.I). The latter predates the small boxed version, and is only known to exist in a single example."[3] As Hendricks indicates, assigning exact dates to a Fluxus edition may not be feasible. There are at least three dates that are relevant for the art historical record: the year the artist created the prototype, the year the edition was produced, and the year when the actual copy of the edition saw the light of day.[4] In addition, Maciunas's charts may sometimes fail as a reliable source, and dating when a copy was produced often involves guesswork.

Putting aside questions of the singularity and exact genealogy of *Zen for Film*'s versions for the moment, it must be noted that the early screening of Paik's empty leader may have been linear rather than looped. Cage's recollection of a "one-hour-long imageless film" might be interpreted either way (as a linear projection lasting one hour or a looped projection watched in a one-hour-long session); the records of Maciunas's correspondence from *Fluxus Codex* point, however, to a linear variant of the film. Similarly, Mekas recalls that for the screenings in the Cinematheque, he installed a 16mm projector that ran a 30-minute film in a linear rather than looped manner.[5] Still uncertain as to its looped or linear character, art historians do assume that the film was reused. Jenkins describes the Fluxhall version of the film: "Visible already were the scratches and dust particles that would continue to accumulate on the print, injecting new content into and onto subsequent screenings."[6] The accumulative character of the initial film was arrested with its consecration as a relic, as a film remnant from the 1960s that must have resulted from the decision to replace the filmstrips for each subsequent display of the artwork.[7] But is some other kind of film relic perhaps possible?

The looped version of *Zen for Film* may have occurred as a way to optimize the process of projection. It is equally possible that it emerged as a result of Maciunas's pragmatic vision of distributing *Zen for Film* as a "do-it-yourself" Fluxus edition. Why send around an entire film canister if one could screen the film using a much shorter loop? After all, a short loop costs less, which reconfirms Fluxus's conviction that art should be made of economically obtainable materials (Maciunas acquired the generic boxes for the editions on Canal Street).[8] Nevertheless, although Maciunas clearly speaks of "looped" versions of Fluxfilms, the "loopers"—projectors that enable a looped presentation of a film—do not appear to have become readily available until later.[9]

A number of excerpts from European Mail-Order Warehouse advertisements, Maciunas's letters, and newspaper clippings offer some evidence regarding the film's duration, type of projection, and length of leader.[10] For instance, in

1964 and 1965 *Zen for Film* was offered as a 20-minute 16mm version[11] or as variable lengths of 20 and 30 minutes, and as a 44-minute variant.[12] In February 1965, the work becomes an "indefinite length"[13] and is mentioned as a loop in summer 1964 and March 1965.[14] Later, *Zen for Film* is increasingly "boxed" and looped; it is distributed as a Fluxus edition, or shown as either a linear or looped version.[15] As already mentioned, the collective Fluxus editions that include *Zen for Film* are Fluxkits (such as "A" and "B" versions, both packaged as black attaché cases).[16] Paik's film is missing, however, from the Year Box 2, which was the principal compilation of Fluxfilms.

Against the common view that Fluxus acted against the regime of the art market and institutions of display, the emergence of the editioned, boxed variant of *Zen for Film* might be seen as an act of facilitating its distribution to, and accommodation by, collections. And yet the development of the edition model through the twentieth century, which becomes a common form of circulation of "moving-image art," limits and channels its distribution.[17] Shifting from the circulation of unrestricted copies to a prescribed imposition of scarcity, the idea of editioned film and video in the twentieth century looks back to the multiple casts of nineteenth-century bronze sculptures. Indeed, the rise of reproducibility, Walter Benjamin argues, came to threaten the aura and uniqueness of art.[18] This, in turn, reinforces the valorization of originality, scarcity, and authenticity. The copy, according to American art critic Rosalind Krauss, becomes the "underlying condition of the original";[19] in other words, originality emerges from the possibility of the existence of a copy. Therefore, the "originality" of *Zen for Film*'s remnant from the 1960s might be regarded as an attempt to withstand the infinite reproducibility of the film as a projection and as a Fluxfilm edition; the remnant might potentially be limited to the presumed existence of a number of exemplars (although in fact only one is known to exist, extant in the Silverman collection) rather than limited by Maciunas from the outset. In terms of fixing *Zen for Film* as an artifact (and disregarding the properties of the film projection that might result from it), the Fluxfilm edition is ordered, rendered countable, and, at least to a certain degree, assigned a provenance—an authorship and origin. Although, to be sure, one could easily assemble a blank film just like Paik's on a home projector, its scarcity is marked by the presence of both the Fluxus edition and the film remnant, giving them, as with a traditional art object, an aura of uniqueness. As I will explain in the next revision, because *Zen for Film* eludes the material identity of a specific iteration (if one assumes that all it needs is mounting a blank film on a projector), the museum establishes a convention based on a consensus that follows traditional paradigms for protecting the uniqueness of an object. Within such paradigms, limitless distribution would diminish its value.

Notes

1—Along with Paik, *Concert No. 5* featured artists such as Brecht, Philip Corner, Higgins, Toshi Ichiyanagi, György Ligeti, Maciunas, and Tomas Schmit. *Zen for Film* is also mentioned as a part of *20 Fluxfilms* at the Anthology Film Archives, New York, on April 5, 1977, and on July 9 and 10, 1977, as a part of the never-realized *Flux Fest: Nature* in New Marlborough, Massachusetts. Hendricks's anthology ends with the death of Maciunas in 1978.

2—This mention is confirmed in *Film Culture,* no. 43 (Winter 1966), which lists *Zen for Film* as follows: "Nam June Paik ZEN FOR FILM, 1962–64 realized by Fluxus, 30 min. rental: $10." Maciunas also dates the film to 1962–64.

3—*Fluxus Codex*, 438. Hendricks's description makes no mention of the existence of *Zen for Film—Fluxfilm No. 1*, which was created by Maciunas together with other Fluxfilms and assembled into *Fluxfilm Anthology* and Fluxfilm programs. See "The Film" section of the introduction.

4—Hendricks, *Fluxus Etc. / Addenda II*, 4; hereafter *Addenda II.*

5—Mekas, discussion with the author.

6—Jenkins, "Fluxfilm in Three False Starts," 68.

7—According to John Hanhardt, consulting senior curator at the Smithsonian American Art Museum, during the preparations for his exhibition at the Guggenheim Museum (*The Worlds of Nam June Paik*, February 11–April 26, 2000), Paik threw the filmstrip on the floor, maintaining that it should collect traces. Hanhardt, in discussion with the author, March 2015. This anecdote implies the practice of replacing the leader rather than consecrating its physical state; the "relic" would not have been treated this way.

8—These economic considerations are somewhat at odds with Kellein's assertion that *Zen for Film* was also produced in a luxury edition on sale for "the extraordinarily high price of fifty dollars." Kellein, *The Dream of Fluxus*, 106.

9—Continuous loop projectors were not part of the avant-garde art scene of the 1960s. Years later, when artists such as Rodney Graham and Tacita Dean wanted to loop their work, loopers were custom-made. Barbara London (former associate curator, MoMA, New York), discussion with the author, December 2012 and December 2014. Bill Brand (experimental filmmaker, educator, and preservationist) recalls that Paul Sharits, with whom he collaborated on the installation of his first looped film installation, *Film Strip / Sound Strip* (1972, using Super 8mm Fairchild projectors), was excited to find new possibilities for looping 16mm film—perhaps an indication of the scarcity of this technology in the late 1960s and early 1970s. Brand, discussion with the author, February 2015.

10—The European Mail-Order Warehouse / Fluxshop, maintained by Willem de Ridder in his private apartment in Amsterdam and later acquired by the Silvermans, was responsible for mailing dozens of Fluxus editions.

11—The 30-minute variant was offered for $50; its looped version, for $3. European Mail-Order Warehouse / Fluxshop, notes from Maciunas to de Ridder, quoted in *Fluxus Codex*, 437, and *Vacuum TRapEzoid: Fluxus Newspaper*, no. 5 (March 1965).

12—On July 21, 1964, Maciunas wrote to Ben Vautier: "You could now easily make a FLUXUS film festival with 4 films: 1. Paik's *Zen for film* (transparent blank film) about 20 or 50 minutes." *Fluxus Codex*, 437; original spelling. A 30-minute version that might rent for $10 is announced in *Film Culture*, no. 43 (Winter 1966). In *Fluxnewsletter*, December 2, 1968 (revised March 15, 1969), *Zen for Film* becomes not only 44 minutes long but is dated 1963. See *Fluxus Codex*, 438.

13—In a later letter by Maciunas addressed to Vautier (February 1, 1965), we read: "I have asked Barbara Moore to send you 2 films, Paik's *Zen for film*. . . . Make loops from them and then you can show them for an indefinite length, OK?" *Fluxus Codex*, 438.

14—Notes from Maciunas to de Ridder. Ibid. *Vacuum TRapEzoid* mentions "FLUXUS gz NAM JUNE PAIK: zen for film 16mm loop, in plastic box $3," offering Paik's film as a part of a Fluxkit or separately. *Vacuum TRapEzoid Newspaper*, no. 5 (March 1965); original spelling.

15—For instance, during the exhibition *Happening und Fluxus* at Kölnische Kunstverein in Cologne (November 6, 1970–January 6, 1971, curated by Hanns Sohm and Harald Szeemann), Paik's film was present as a 44-minute 16mm variant (no date indication) and as a "boxed" film leader, Fluxus Edition, dated 1964. Sohm, *Happening und Fluxus*, n.p.

16—Whereas many boxed *Zen for Film* editions simply include a clear leader of varying length, the leader of *Zen for Film* from the Fluxkit of the Silverman Fluxus collection, which resembles "Flux-Kit ('B' copy)" (as listed in *Fluxus Etc.*), is already looped.
17—See Balsom, "Original Copies," 98.
18—See Benjamin, "The Work of Art in the Age of Its Technological Reproducibility," 101–33.
19—Krauss, "The Originality of the Avant-Garde," 162.

5th Revision—

How to Exhibit a Work and Its World?

I think that we are missing the art for the trees.
—Jon Hendricks

When it comes to the moment of exhibiting *Zen for Film*, the standard line of inquiry may not be sufficient to account for the challenges posed by it—and not simply because the general characteristics of an iterant, changeable artwork require that presentation and conservation questions go hand in hand in order to account for its visuality and materiality. In fact, presentation questions never exhaust the technical and philosophical complexities of conservation and preservation work. Although it is accepted practice to obtain permission before *Zen for Film* can be exhibited, Paik's work is simply not in fact *exhibitable* without asking more profound questions about its nature and behavior. In this revision, I will provide some evidence for this claim.

But let us start at the beginning of the process. Among the many ways to display *Zen for Film*, perhaps the simplest involves obtaining permission to project an empty film leader. Permission could be requested from the Nam June Paik Estate, MoMA, the Centre Pompidou in Paris, or from a number of other museums or collections.[1] Although permission from the Paik estate lacks formal specifications, MoMA includes explicit instructions. When someone wishes to borrow *Zen for Film*, MoMA stipulates that it is lending only the use of a concept. No physical object changes hands.[2] In the past, MoMA has lent a film canister containing an early version of the film—designated as a relic—to be shown in a nearby vitrine, offering the possibility of displaying two different things—*Zen for Film* as a projection and a film canister and its contents. Although the canister was often exhibited (as in the Guggenheim exhibition described in revision 1), MoMA's recent policy discourages presenting the container because it is not now considered integral to the artwork (compare fig. 10 to fig. 20).[3] MoMA also specifies that the borrower is responsible for obtaining a projector and a looped 16mm blank film leader of any length.[4] Finally, the museum prohibits exhibiting the film simultaneously in two locations—a restriction corroborated by the Paik estate—though if *Zen for Film* is unavailable (presumably because it is on display or on loan elsewhere), the museum has lent *Zen for Film* from Fluxkit in its place.[5]

The specified display for *Zen for Film* from Fluxkit requires closer attention, as these instructions differ. Though again, the borrower is charged with procuring the film leader to be used during the installation, MoMA requires further that this leader must measure 8mm instead of 16mm and that the plastic box of the Fluxus edition "must be shown alongside the installation."[6] Compare this to the Walker Art Center in Minneapolis, which has used a 16mm variant from the *Zen for Film* Fluxus edition in its own collection (*Art Expanded, 1958–1978*, June 14, 2014–March 1, 2015; fig. 21). The implicit assumption that the film leader from the Fluxus edition is not projectable makes it, in a sense, yet another relic similar to the one enclosed in the canister, although multiplied in a number of existing editions.

Another question pertains to the actual difference between the visual appearance of the 16mm and 8mm variants of the film projection itself. Even projectors for films of the same size differ among themselves. If the work cannot be exhibited in two locations simultaneously, while the only criterion of verification is the size of the film leader, how can we define what is different in the produced image without taking the materiality of display into account? How can we educate viewers, and how can viewers know the difference between the projections while contemplating the work? Are the wall label and the presence of a Fluxfilm box enough to create a significant difference? And, last but not least, why does it matter?

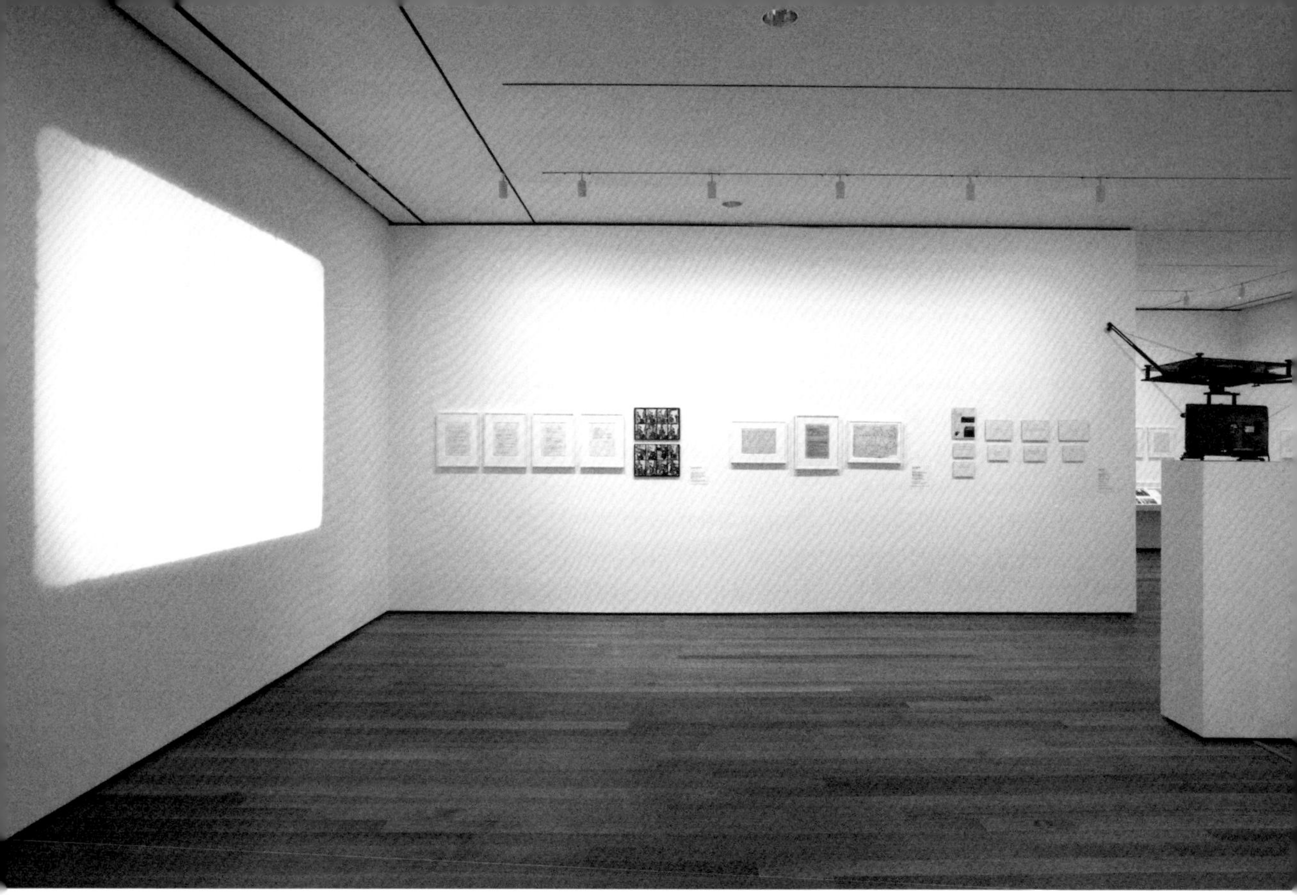

Fig. 20—*Zen for Film* installation in *There Will Never Be Silence: Scoring John Cage's 4′33″*. Museum of Modern Art, October 12, 2013–June 22, 2014. Photograph by Jonathan Muzikar. The Museum of Modern Art, New York. © The Museum of Modern Art / Licensed by SCALA / Art Resource, NY.

According to Jon Huffman, curator of the Paik estate, the coexistence of two film projections in close proximity—for instance, within the geographical terrain of the city of New York—is indeed unacceptable.[7] The dilemma of the sameness of projection coincides with the simultaneity of existence of *Zen for Film* not only in multiple collections but also within a single one. The MoMA collection holds three boxed editions of *Zen for Film*. Does prohibiting simultaneous projection of *Zen for Film* also apply to the projection of the editions, if there are three of them in one collection? Certainly, the nature of an edition is inherently plural, and yet there is a sense of disapproval hovering over the multiple existences of *Zen for Film* at the museum—the scenario of a polyphonic symphony of projections can be imagined as a consequence. Does traditional museum practice fail to accommodate the complexity of *Zen for Film*? Is our thinking too deeply rooted in the metaphysics of the static, unique object?

Rather than criticizing individual institutional practices or personal perspectives, my account addresses the paradox of multiplicity so as to point to the complexity of the institutional life of this kind of work. Hypothetically, a projection of MoMA's *Zen for Film* 16mm might coincide with a projection of the same variant at the Centre Pompidou, and at the same time a projection of the Walker Art Center's *Zen for Film* 16mm from Fluxkit might coincide with a projection from MoMA's Fluxkit version in New York. But would these variants be *exactly* the same if nothing changes hands but instructions, formulated or implied? In fact, the prohibition against the simultaneous display of *Zen for Film* remains largely unenforceable because the Fluxus edition has ended up in many private as well as other institutional collections.

And let us return to the requirement that the film must be looped. Most likely the instruction stems from a later development in the life of the artwork.

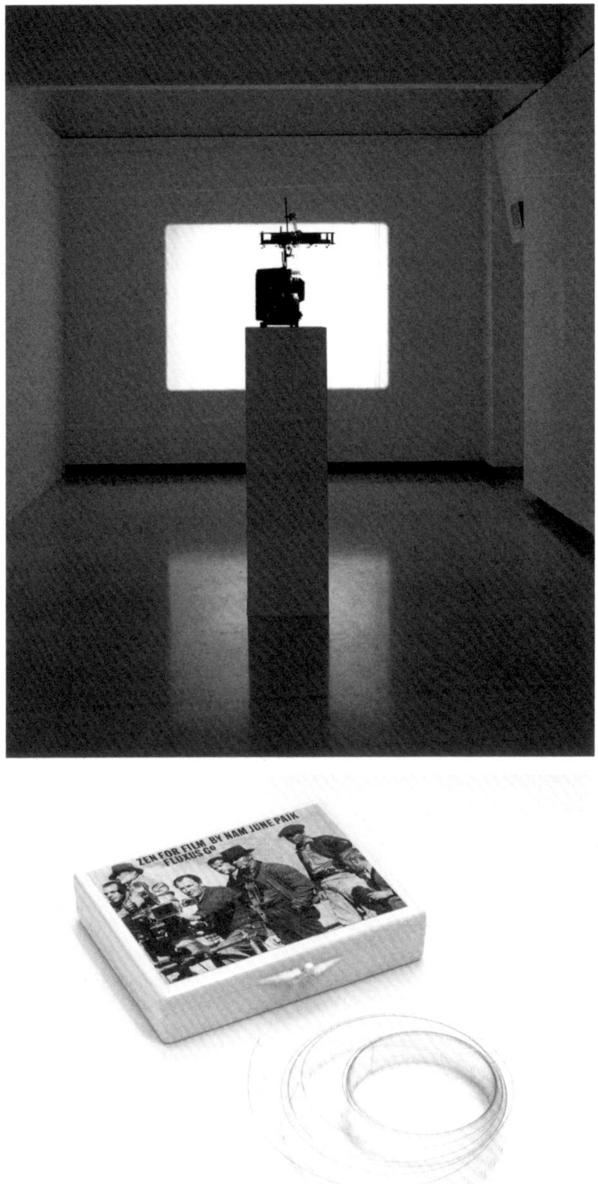

Fig. 21—Top: *Zen for Film* installation in *Art Expanded, 1958–1978*. Walker Art Center, June 14, 2014–March 1, 2015. Walker Art Center. Bottom: Nam June Paik. *Zen for Film*, 1964. Assembled and designed by George Maciunas. Plastic box with offset label, containing blank film loop. Walker Art Center, Walker Special Purchase Fund, 1989, 1989.303.1–.2 © 2015 Nam June Paik Estate.

As we have seen, a looped variant of *Zen for Film* was produced sometime after the linear projection initially conceived by Paik. Regardless of the genealogy of variants, the implications of the shift from linearity to circularity are ontological. This shift marks the transition from the spectacle of a cinematic event with determined points of beginning and end to an undetermined temporality based on circularity, indeterminacy of spectatorship, and a different mode of accumulating traces. Although including a linear mode of projection in *Zen for Film*'s repertoire would be reasonable, it would not guarantee an optimal solution, given that the freedom in handling *Zen for Film*'s concept may, as mentioned earlier, result in looping the digitized linear version of *Zen for Film* from *Fluxfilm Anthology*.

Yet another aspect of the troubled existence of *Zen for Film* is the status of the film leader and the canister in which it is contained as relics. An object—often a tangible memorial such as the physical remains of a saint or the saint's personal effects preserved for purposes of veneration—becomes a relic through a process of authentication, official designation, or both. In fact, there is no certainty that the film canister was ever touched by Paik's hand, which perhaps explains why the museum now discourages presenting the canister alongside the film projection. Yet when it comes to displaying the 8mm film, the box of the edition (fig. 22a) *must* be shown in direct proximity to the projector (fig. 22b). Why should the canister containing the 16mm film reel not be granted privileged status next to the work being exhibited, while the Fluxbox is deemed crucial to understanding the work? Although there is no evidence to suggest that Paik ever assigned his authorial seal to these Fluxboxes, perhaps Maciunas did. To be sure, both the Fluxbox and the film canister undoubtedly connect us to the past and signal that the film being shown comes from the container or has a relationship to the box, even though we know that the film being projected is not the same film that sits safely in cold storage or dormant in its case.

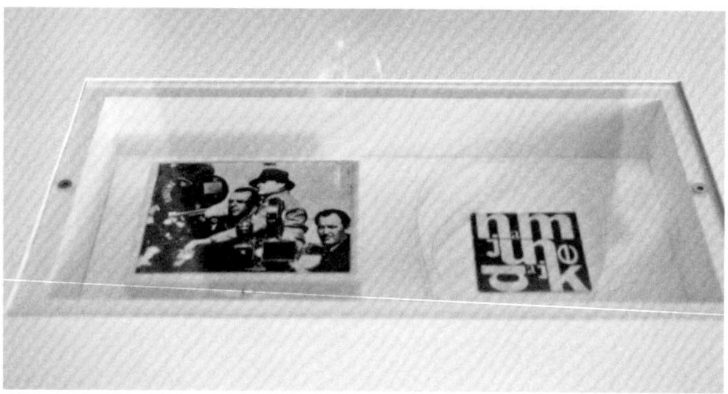

Fig. 22a—*Zen for Film* installation in *Art of Its Own Making*. Pulitzer Arts Foundation, St. Louis, February 14–August 20, 2014. Fluxbox, presented alongside the projection, Museum of Modern Art, New York, The Gilbert and Lila Silverman Collection Gift, 2008. Photograph by David Johnson. Pulitzer Arts Foundation.

Last but not least, looking closer at the logic that lies behind the preservation of the film remnant, should the preservation of all film leaders that have ever run through a projector as *Zen for Film* be encouraged? Although the museum suggests that all used film leaders should be destroyed, we may nonetheless hypothesize that, if all of them were collected (and I am convinced—given the multiple existences of the film in collections—that some, in fact, have been), this would create an immense archive of physical traces and palpable cinematic temporality ready to be activated in the future.

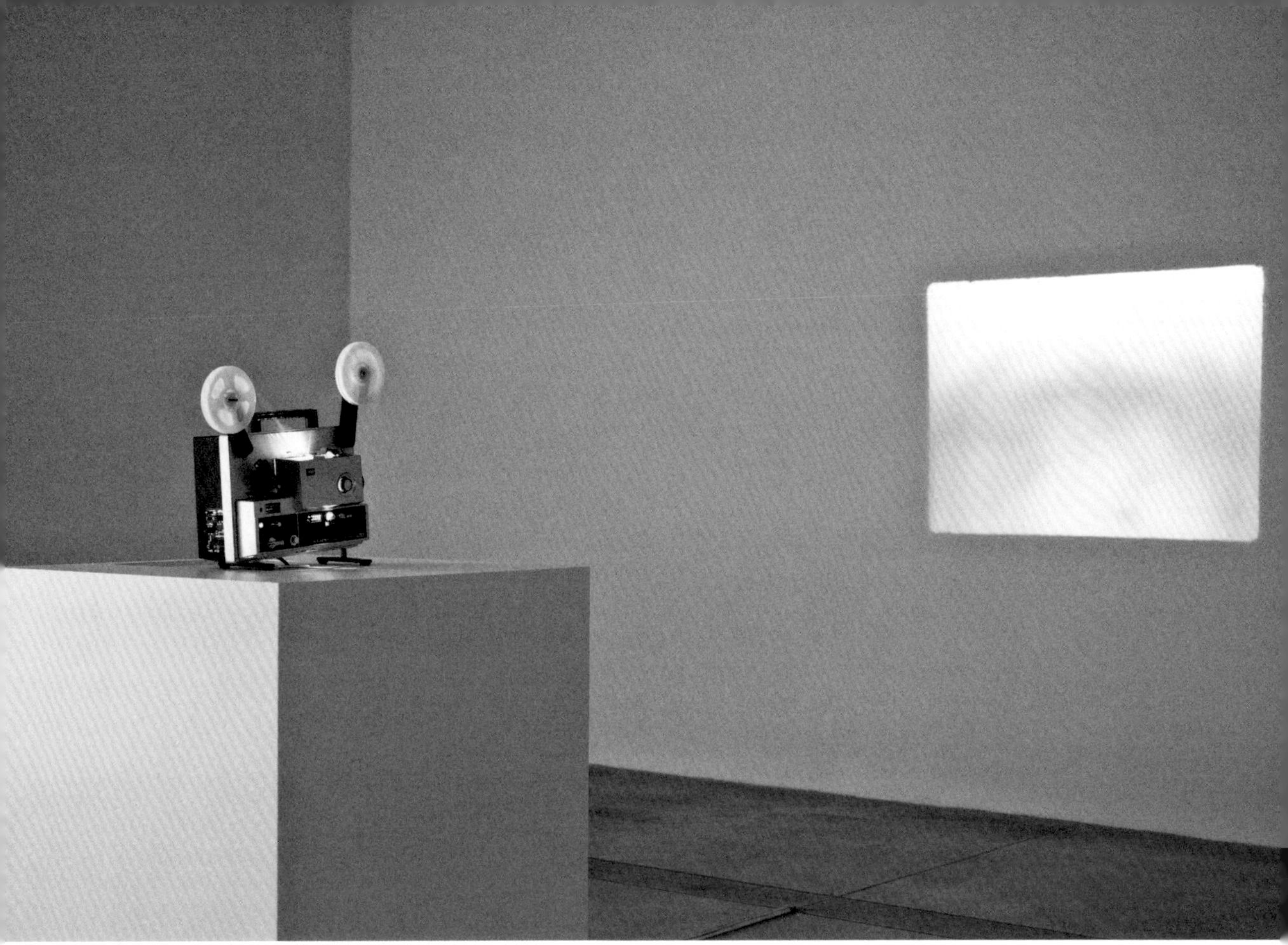

Fig. 22b—*Zen for Film* installation in *Art of Its Own Making*. Pulitzer Arts Foundation, St. Louis, February 14–August 20, 2014. Projection of Fluxus edition, Museum of Modern Art, New York, The Gilbert and Lila Silverman Collection Gift, 2008. Photograph by David Johnson. Pulitzer Arts Foundation.

The entanglement of visuality and materiality in Paik's *Zen for Film* raises questions that strain rational thinking about exhibitable objects. As a global, open work, *Zen for Film* is determined only by instructions, either implied or, at times, produced by museums. What exactly is the function of an instruction? Does it satisfy the economics of circulation, in that it facilitates the reinstantiation of the film in different venues? Does it sufficiently valorize the film as "object"?[8] Indeed, we might go so far as to ask *why* permission must be granted to display *Zen for Film* at all. Is the work not a concept, its object-sphere merely an artifactual anchor of its floating identity, a museum prop, or a leftover that secures the work's status as a collectable commodity?

The possibility of multiple spatial and temporal existences of *Zen for Film*—as in the case of other changeable artworks—goes beyond the established systems of classification and ensures that the conditions for its continuation might not be limited either by institutional or individual sanctions. The major challenge that arises with the moment of archiving, presenting, and conserving *Zen for Film* is to avoid sacrificing its changeable character.

Notes

1—I encountered these first three listed options during my research; however, a loan inquiry to other institutions that own *Zen for Film*, such as Harvard Art Museums / Fogg Museum, the Walker Art Center in Minneapolis, and many private collections, might yield even more diverse results. As a rule, in current practice, permissions granted by a collection (and usually related to a physical manifestation of the work) are additionally accompanied by an inquiry to the Paik estate, whereas museums holding the artwork do not usually seek permission from the estate to project it.

2—As per MoMA's preliminary *Zen for Film* loan specifications, obtained by the author in October 2014.

3—MoMA has now removed the film from circulation altogether. It is currently preserved in cold storage because of degradation of the film substrate.

4—*Zen for Film* loan specifications, October 2014.

5—The MoMA *Zen for Film* from Fluxkit (2627.2008.a-c) is probably the one George Maciunas produced in 1965, after having announced it in the fourth Fluxus newspaper, *Fluxus cc five ThReE*, in 1964.

6—Loan Agreement for *Zen for Film* from Fluxkit from MoMA to Bard Graduate Center Gallery, April 23, 2015. *The Art of Its Own Making* exhibition at the Pulitzer Arts Foundation, St. Louis (February 14–August 20, 2014) included an example of a *Zen for Film* from Fluxkit displayed with an 8mm leader; see figs. 22a–b). As the present volume was being researched and written in 2015, MoMA'a *Zen for Film* from Fluxkit was still thought to contain an 8mm film leader. In July 2015, MoMA revised the 8mm listing to 16mm. This example further illustrates how *Zen for Film* continues to evade accurate description and how providing instructions for such a work can be complicated.

7—Jon Huffman, telephone conversation with Nina Stritzler-Levine, Bard Graduate Center gallery director, March 2015. Nevertheless, one must still wonder to what degree the restriction reflects the artist's own intentions. Was Paik himself interested in limiting projections in close proximity? This must remain an open question.

8—For questions concerning the economics of circulation of film and video, see Balsom, "Original Copies."

6th Revision—

The Dualism of Concept and Material

Because *Zen for Film* is constantly changing form, material, and context, the film enjoys a largely ambiguous status. At times, as I have shown, it is distributed as a film to be spun on the spools of a projector (Maciunas rented it for festivals), at times lent as a concept (by various collections, including the Paik estate), and at times displayed as a boxed artifact valued for its origins (Fluxus editions from various collections and the filmic relic).

Certainly, if *Zen for Film* were to be conceptualized as a cinematic spectacle, its vehicular medium[1] would play a less significant role and would be regarded as merely the physical carrier of the artistic idea. But such an assumption would be a simplification. Indeed, *Zen for Film*'s vehicular medium might also become the artifact(s) valued for the history of its origins—an object, a remnant or relic to be preserved. This complicates not only the understanding of what the work is but also the ways in which it is approached within collections.

As we have seen, when *Zen for Film* is distributed as a concept to be actualized on the basis of a set of instructions (score, notation, or loan specifications), it materializes anew regardless of the medium's material origins. In other words, neither the projection apparatus nor the film leader retains its historic or evidentiary character as "authentic" in the sense of material authenticity and history of production. These characteristics of *Zen for Film* enable us to test the applicability of two conceptual frameworks: musical performance, of which each instance is a genuine piece of work independent of the number of its iterations, and conceptual art, which allows an artwork to exist in a series of materializations based on instructions. This revision, then, reexamines the duality of concept and material in *Zen for Film*.

In contrast to traditional artworks, the nature of which generally relies on the persistence of their identity in their original material, *Zen for Film* assumes its physical shape only when it is installed. This means that the work exists intermittently as a material and conceptual entity, sharing these characteristics—as do a number of multimedia installations—with conceptual artworks. Because the borrower of *Zen for Film* requests only use of the concept, the work materializes anew every time it is exhibited but otherwise has no physical existence.

Although the concept takes precedence over the material in conceptual art,[2] a number of conceptual artworks share *Zen for Film*'s instability. Ono's *Instructions for Paintings* (created for the Sogetsu Art Center, Tokyo, May 1962)—one of the first forms of conceptual art in which the instructions "summarize the painting-events in a way that makes them repeatable"[3]—parallel the variety of instantiations of Paik's film. Along with the potential for simultaneous existence in different locations, both the paintings resulting from Ono's instructions and *Zen for Film* convey a certain lack of concern regarding the preservation of their material embodiment.

Zen for Film's distribution specifications, issued by Maciunas and later reformulated into MoMA's instructions, locate the artwork in the ideological proximity of conceptual art. The instructions convey the concept of the artwork, revised by a collection that harbors it, usually within the curatorial or registration department responsible for processing loan requests. Besides its contractual role and practical function of providing information regarding the artwork's installation, the instructions become a form of conceptual stabilization of a work in the absence of physical material. The certificate, for instance, issued when Paik's *TV Garden* (1974) was acquired by the Nam June Paik Art Center in Seoul, constitutes a set of instructions. As with conceptual art, although the artwork may only be experienced in an installed condition, this document stands for the artwork in its (physical) absence, providing legal and tangible evidence of its existence.

On a certain level of materiality, in its recurrent appearance and disappearance as a physical object, *Zen for Film* conjoins Fluxus's and conceptualism's antipathy toward the fetishized object and the accompanying processes of commodification.[4] The links between Fluxus and conceptualism were established as early as the beginning of the 1960s (evident, for instance, in Henry Flynt's and George Brecht's art), although they remained outside art world discourse until almost a decade later.[5]

The idea of bringing together *Zen for Film* and conceptual art may well be viewed with a critical eye. To my knowledge, Paik's *Zen for Film* never existed as a pure set of instructions that excluded the possibility of their realization, nor was it conceived in the spirit of the elimination of the art object or in accord with Joseph Kosuth's emphasis on art as idea.[6] Despite its repeated (and repetitive) dematerialization,[7] *Zen for Film* becomes what it is because it is realized and because it materializes, physically.

My claim regarding the ideological connection between conceptual art and Paik's film stems from the conviction that it is impossible to isolate Paik's oeuvre entirely from the conceptual tendencies of the 1960s. Artists, like their artworks, are never islands enclosed in the solitude of creation. *Zen for Film* and conceptual art participate in the same post-Cagean ontological shift—the general change since the 1960s in the concept of art, of what art can be. Conceptual art and Paik's *Zen for Film* both provoke similar questions regarding their presentation and conservation, questions related to the cyclical repeatability of their materializations and the relative importance of their material traces.

Notes

1—The analytic philosopher David Davies distinguishes between the "physical" or "vehicular" (paint and canvas, body) and the "artistic" medium (brush strokes, articulated steps). According to Davies, artistic statement is articulated through the artistic medium in part and through the manipulation of the vehicular medium. The artistic medium mediates between what the artist does and what the work says. Davies, *Art as Performance,* 58–59. In my account, I use the term "vehicular medium" as the equivalent of a physical carrier (a term frequently employed in media conservation).

2—Sol LeWitt maintains that "in conceptual art the idea or concept is the most important aspect of the work. When an artist uses a conceptual form of art, it means that all of the planning and decisions are made beforehand and the execution is a perfunctory affair. The idea becomes a machine that makes the art." LeWitt, "Paragraphs on Conceptual Art," 79.

3—Osborne, *Conceptual Art*, 21.

4—See Dezeuze, "Play, Ritual and Politics," 220.

5—For the development of conceptualism, see also Bird and Newman, introduction to *Rewriting Conceptual Art,* 1–11.

6—See Kosuth, "Art after Philosophy."

7—Differing from Lucy Lippard's treatment of the art historical valency of the idea of "dematerialization" (see Lippard, *Six Years*), my use of this term leans toward the cyclical principle of de- and rematerialization of installation artworks, which mark different stages in their trajectories.

7th Revision—

Musical Connotations

Conceptualism is further linked with music by the presence of instructions and a score, which are, according to Peter Osborne, a significant contribution of modernist music to conceptual art.[1] Osborne maintains that Cage extended the notion of a score and moved away from the score as a self-sufficient musical entity to other aspects of performance and then back to an expanded conception of the score.[2] In George Brecht's event scores, which Osborne describes as "generalized, and transposed into the medium of language," the score becomes a set of instructions.[3]

It might be useful at this moment to recall Paik's musical background; his education and early career in experimental music were prominently inspired by Cage and Karlheinz Stockhausen.[4] His studies with German composer Wolfgang Fortner and activities in the electronic studio at West German radio station WDR in Cologne, an important center for contemporary music that attracted composers such as Mauricio Kagel, György Ligeti, and Stockhausen, shaped Paik's attitude toward creative practice. Nonetheless, Paik did not feel accepted in this field. "Basically I wasn't a good composer. I got by, because people liked the idea of someone from an underdeveloped country composing in the style of Stockhausen. But if I have any talent, it's a higher demand for perfection than most people have.

I don't want to be a second rate Stockhausen," he stated.[5] The concepts of indeterminacy and chance explored by Cage—and later also inherent in Fluxus—significantly influenced Paik. He took Cage's instrumentation—the implementation of prepared pianos, audiotapes, and radio receivers as musical instruments—rather seriously. What separated Paik from Cage—and became important in his transition from music to visual arts—was that Paik saw those instruments as objects with visual qualities rather than as mere apparatuses responsible for the production of noise. This attitude would not only result in his aesthetic treatment of objects as a sort of instrumentation but also in his conception of their afterlives. In Paik's words:

> Video installation will become like Opera . . . in which only the score will be *ueberliefert* [passed on] to the next generation and the video curators in the next and subsequent generations will [reinterpret] and install them every time new in their *anpassendes* [adapted] Place and the accents of the new incarnation will have the strong personal traits of the conductor, like Karajan's Neunte or Toscanini's Dritte.[6]

The composer and musicologist Michael Nyman recalls that in his letter to Cage, Paik expressed his pride in not working with "graphically notated scores."[7] The unrealized project *Symphony for 20 Rooms* (1961), however, is known today only from a written score. And a number of Paik's works, such as *Moon Is the Oldest TV* (1965), *TV Clock* (1963), and *TV Buddha* (1974), are oriented around written or oral instructions that have been and can be materialized anew, unbound to any specific material.[8] To my knowledge, Paik did not formulate a written score for *Zen for Film*, which returns us to the paradox of the loan politics discussed in revision 5.

Zen for Film undergoes a process of constant reinterpretation that recalls Paik's comparison of video installations to opera. The film perpetually seeks new embodiments in response to curatorial concepts, gallery space, and available resources. Instructions strive to stabilize the work on a conceptual level, while freeing the work from becoming fixed in a certain physical materiality. From the perspective of the continuation of *Zen for Film*'s life, this lack of fixity runs against the tenets of traditional conservation practice, which preserves material manifestations of an object in the best state possible. Abandoning any care for material origins and material "uniqueness," it renders the work fleeting from one occurrence to the next, liberating it from material gravity and thus guaranteeing its survival.

In this new sense of continuity through performance, there is no place for repetition, because, according to Paik, it is precisely repetition that makes for a bad (and boring) performance. Paik's aversion to repetition stands in clear opposition, however, to his attitude toward replication. One study reveals that around one-third of Paik's artworks that entered museum collections had already been reproduced before they were acquired and that nowadays every second work of Paik's cannot claim the status of being a unique object.[9] In fact, the motif of repetition and iteration is woven throughout Paik's oeuvre, testing assumptions about the singular status of many of his works.[10] But what exactly does it mean for an artwork to be "non-unique" or "unsingular"?

Notes

1—Osborne, *Conceptual Art*, 21.
2—Ibid.
3—Ibid.
4—For a genealogy of Paik's musical engagements, see Nyman, "Nam June Paik, Composer," 79.
5—Truman, "Set Pieces," 184.
6—Original spelling. Paik, "Artificial Intelligence vs Artificial Metabolism," 252–53.
7—Nyman, "Nam June Paik, Composer," 79.
8—See Hölling, "*Re*:Paik," 65–70.
9—See Kim, *Nam June Paik*, 64.
10—The idea of an object as a series of iterations rather than as a singular entity and the relation between repetition and reproduction are both worth considering, particularly in terms of "recursion," a term derived from linguistics, cybernetics, and computer science. In contrast to iteration (the process of repeating an action or object an arbitrary number of times, with each repetition a separate act that can exist apart from the others), recursion involves embedding the action or object within another instance of itself (for instance, a painting of a painting of a painting). In art criticism and cultural studies, the idea of recursion has been taken up by Rosalind Krauss (*A Voyage on the North Sea,* 2000) in relation to the notion of medium as a recursive structure capable of specifying itself, and by Pamela M. Lee (*Chronophobia,* 2004) in terms of a model of temporality in the postwar era that impacted the art of the 1960s. For recursion in linguistics, see Kinsella, "Was Recursion the Key Step?"

8th Revision—

Originality, Authenticity, *Wirkung*

Written instructions and performance complicate the concept of "uniqueness" associated with the singularity of the visual art object. But because Paik's creative process was guided by original ideas, classifying his works as non-unique is inadequate; rather, his art shifts away from the uniqueness of an object toward the originality of the idea, as it does in conceptual art in general.

For decades, considerable attention has been given to the idea of originality and the authenticity of objects. Not unproblematic, especially in conservation, these concepts revolve around the material understanding of an artwork in relation to its vehicular, physical medium and its origins—the empirical facts deriving from the history of its production. More recent artistic projects, however, present conservation with the problem of the inadaptability of these concepts to changeable artworks. For *Zen for Film*, thinking along the lines of material authenticity confronts a paradox: if the work sheds the physical carriage of its materials and is installed every time anew, how can one still speak of its material authenticity?

A solution to this problem might be provided by theories of musical performance.[1] American philosopher Denis Dutton discusses the presentation of art through the example of Western notated music: as a two-stage process, the creation of music diverges from other forms of visual, plastic arts, such as painting and sculpture.[2] A work of classical music is specified by a score, a set of instructions "realized aurally by performers, normally for the pleasure of audiences."[3] Performances may differ markedly because of the nature of the score, leaving a space for translation from the written encoded language of the score to the sound of the realization of the performance. One philosopher of music, Stephen Davies, identifies different types of interpretation of musical scores according to the degree of accuracy with which the performer follows the script. The very idea of performance is thus permissive toward the interpretive freedom "consistent with conventions that govern what counts as properly following the score."[4] Davies's point might be well illustrated by the example of the recordings of Canadian pianist Glenn Gould's interpretations of Johann Sebastian Bach's *Goldberg Variations* (the first in 1955, the second in 1981). Although the difference between them is remarkable, both interpretations have become an intrinsic part of the history of music.

Although some of Paik's works and media installations remain "performed" (in the sense of musical performance), while others are sculptural, the *Zen for Film* projection clearly denies a material, nominal authenticity that relies on empirical facts associated with the artwork's origins and history of production. Rather, *Zen for Film* projection might be characterized by "expressive authenticity," which concerns the quality of interpretation,[5] the "faithfulness to the performer's own self"[6] following a set of instructions, and which might be applied to the performed part of an installation. A historically authentic performance may involve employing either historical or new instrumentation.

But how can we determine whether, for instance, playing Bach on a piano is less "authentic" than playing Bach on a harpsichord? Dutton insists that historic authenticity provides no guarantee of achieving a full realization of the score's aesthetic potential. The American musicologist Richard Taruskin makes a similar point, claiming that a historical performance using historical hardware is never historical, but this is also precisely what makes a musical composition deathless.[7] According to Taruskin, the term "authenticity" in musical performance is a romantic, nineteenth-century inheritance that arose with "museum ideology" and the concept of *Werktreue* (fidelity to the musical work), in which the *Werk* is the "objectified musical work-thing" to which fidelity is owed.[8] Taruskin argues that today's "historical" performance "is not really historical"; rather, "a specious veneer of historicism clothes a performance style that is completely of our own time, and is in fact the most modern style around."[9] Analogously, *Zen for Film* may thus exist without demanding historical correctness—a certain type of the projecting apparatus and a certain type of film—according to the laws of proper instrumentation.

The idea of historic instrumentation calls to mind the distinction between "high" and "low" intentionality proposed by American philosopher Randall R. Dipert.[10] A new instrument introduced into an orchestra in the past may not be regarded as a novelty today. Therefore, Dipert distinguishes between high- and low-level intention. High-level intention designates the wish to use an instrument that would attract the audience's attention by its novelty; in low-level intention, exactly the same instrument would be used even though it is no longer a novelty.[11] Low-level intentions might thus be concerned with the mere means; high-level intentions, with how the composer implements the medium to achieve a certain effect—the *Wirkung*[12] of the medium—which brings us back to the distinction between the vehicular and the artistic medium.

If we once again reconsider *Zen for Film* at the time of its initial presentations in New York, the film projector might not have drawn any particular attention because audiences were largely familiar with its clattering dynamics. Nowadays, with the ubiquitous presence of digital technologies, displaying a film projector—an obsolete medium—acquires another value, that of memory and nostalgia, a longing for the past (an aspect that is effectively being used by a new generation of artists). For Rosalind Krauss, an obsolete medium is characterized by a redemptive quality—although the 16mm film used in *A Voyage on the North Sea* (1973–74) by Marcel Broodthaers is already outdated, this is exactly what makes it available for art.[13] Consequently, the medium of *Zen for Film* is temporal and historical; it changes its valency, meaning, and potential in relation to the development of other media.

American philosopher Nelson Goodman makes a distinction between autographicity and allographicity that is relevant to a reconsideration of *Zen for Film* and "authenticity."[14] Goodman draws a line between artworks that are autographic, or forgeable, such as paintings, and allographic, or unforgeable, such as musical performances. In contrast with paintings, which can be forged, musical performances may vary in accuracy and quality, but each performance is a genuine instance of the work. Autographic arts thus involve works for which even the most exact duplication cannot be regarded as "genuine." Additionally, Goodman classifies painting as a one-stage work and music as two-stage; the one-stage character of a work of art, however, does not determine its autographic or allographic character. Literature, for example, is not autographic though it is one-stage, and art print(making) is two-stage and yet autographic.

According to Goodman's argument, one of the necessary conditions for a work to be allographic would be the irrelevance of a history of production.[15] Thus, while *Zen for Film*'s projection seems to fit the allographic, two-stage category, the film relic enclosed in the canister would be a one-stage, autographic work. The relic, generated as a result of *Zen for Film*'s allographic performance, became an autographic object when the artist designated the object as a work of art. Although there is no certainty as to the origins of the inscription on the canister, the autographic gesture renders the work "determined" and, in a certain way, complete. According to French philosopher Jacques Derrida, the autographic gesture affixes "a seal of authenticity" to an object that bears a signature from the hand of the subject.[16] Otherwise contingent on the potentially inexhaustible possibility of reproduction, the inscription assigns the film canister a unique status and, at the same time, turns it into a "performative" object.[17] The somewhat paradoxical dualism in *Zen for Film* lies in the film's turning the artwork into performance, on the one hand, while the performance becomes affixed to the performative object, on the other. Although the fulfillment of the autographic moment makes it irreplaceable, would the forgery of the film canister shift its status from a relic to a performance prop? What kind of status might be assigned to the film strips of the currently performed projections? I will return to this problem in the final revision.

Notes

1—My analysis of musical performance is largely determined by the perspective of analytic philosophy rather than cultural musicology (see, for instance, works by music theorists Taruskin [*Text and Act*] and Cook ["Between Process and Product"]).

2—See Dutton, "Authenticity in Art." Dutton follows the idea of one- and two-stage works of art described in Goodman, *Languages of Art,* 114.

3—Dutton, "Authenticity in Art," 265.

4—Davies, quoted in ibid. For the relation of musical performance to interpretation, see also Davies, *Musical Works and Performances.* On the implementation of his theory in conservation studies, see Laurenson, "Authenticity, Change and Loss."

5—Dutton, "Authenticity in Art," 267–68.

6—Kivy, *Authenticities*, quoted in ibid., 267.

7—Taruskin, *Text and Act*, 143. For an extended discussion on historically authentic performance, see Davies, *Philosophy of the Performing Arts*, 74–86.

8—Taruskin, *Text and Act*, 10.

9—Ibid., 102.

10—See Butt, *Playing with History*, 76, 88; Davies, *Musical Works and Performances*, 232.

11—Dipert, "Towards a Genuine Philosophy of the Performing Arts," 182–200.

12—The German word *Wirkung* expresses the way in which the object appears and appeals, operates and behaves, and stands in opposition to the understanding of an object as a material fetish. Wulf Herzogenrath, in discussion with the author, March 2010.

13—Krauss, *A Voyage on the North Sea*, 45. Krauss leans on Walter Benjamin's belief that the emergence of a new technology or social form frees the obsolete object from its utility function.

14—See Goodman, *Languages of Art,* 90–123. Subject to criticism, Goodman continued reformulating his theory over the years. Laurenson should be credited for the first implementation of Goodman's theory in the conservation of media art.

15—Goodman, *Of Mind and Other Matters,* 140, quoted in Pillow, "Did Goodman's Distinction Survive LeWitt?," 379.

16—Derrida, *Copy, Archive, Signature: A Conversation on Photography,* 23.

17—For performativity, see Austin, *How to Do Things with Words.*

9th Revision—

Distributed Authorship

Reflecting on *Zen for Film*'s various materializations inevitably prompts questions about authorial agency. Beginning with Giorgio Vasari and culminating in romanticism, artworks in past centuries were traditionally associated with an expression of autonomous genius enacted in a private space.[1] Such a model was finally, although not exclusively, challenged by artistic practices of the second half of the twentieth century and by the post-structural critique of the idea of "authorship." Fluxus offers a particularly fruitful locus for this debate,[2] which develops from the premise that artistic work involves joint activity within organized networks.[3]

The production, dissemination, and (re)installation of a number of multimedia artworks, including *Zen for Film*, requires the joint effort of curators, conservators, artists' assistants, and technicians. Their interpretive agency plays a substantial role in the creation of an artwork's identity. The artist's role, so it seems, might sometimes be limited to formulating the concept and conditions for the work's initial realization, without active engagement in the execution of the work and in its ongoing life. When it comes to the process of distributing, presenting, collecting, and archiving an artwork, the impact of curatorial and conservation decisions on the identity of the work must be reconsidered. This revision will focus on the artwork's plural transitions and the network of people that contribute to the final/non-final "product," *Zen for Film*.

—

As noted earlier, *Zen for Film* owes its existence as a Fluxfilm to Maciunas's idea of Fluxus editions, which he conceived around 1963 after the first of his several Fluxus manifestos in 1962. His early concept of Fluxus editions led to inexpensive open-ended editions of artists' work, which he planned to expand once more work had been generated. Later Fluxus editions from 1965 might be seen as a continuation of his idea of including inexpensive assemblages of artists' events, scores, concepts, and games. Although these editions contain artworks and concepts by individual artists associated with Fluxus, Maciunas played a central role as editor, compiler, and publisher.[4] With the exception perhaps of Fluxus scores, Maciunas did not refrain from free interpretation of the artists' works, endowing games, gestures, and gags with his own sense of authorial engagement.[5] Therefore, to properly understand these editions, we must grasp their collective, rather than individual, authorship.

As mentioned in revision 4, Maciunas's production of *Zen for Film* for Fluxus Editions dates back to 1964 or 1965. In the Fluxus editions, the film was distributed in different lengths and with varying labels.[6] For instance, Flux-Kit "A" differs from Flux-Kit "B" in its content and labeling. The "A" variant contains two long pieces of clear 16mm film and is missing a label, whereas the "B" variant contains a 16mm film leader with labels located on the lid and on the bottom of the box.[7] The variations are probably the result of their having been conceived and assembled over a long period of time. The editions often reflect Maciunas's personal preferences and the availability of the work, which might have simply disappeared. Exceptions are Fluxus editions produced by the artists themselves, such as George Brecht's *Deck* or Mieko Shiomi's *Endless Box*, and works that only later evolved into Maciunas-produced editions.[8] Maciunas's approach to creating the Fluxus editions becomes evident in his letter to Ben Vautier (January 10, 1966): "Did I mention our 8mm film loops for Fluxus II?? . . . but maybe you would like to do a loop also? 2ft long/8mm (or 4ft/16mm). You can just send me [a] 'script' or tell [me] what to do and I can have the film made."[9] Maciunas was apparently not only a producer of the Fluxus editions of the films (in the sense of Hollywood productions) but also the "maker" of the films.

Can we still claim, when we return to the question of *Zen for Film*'s authorship, that Paik is the sole author of the work in the traditional sense? It should now be clear that the "do-it-yourself" Fluxkit version of *Zen for Film* was created and produced by Maciunas rather than Paik. If the vehicular medium serves only as a carrier of an artistic idea, and the artistic medium remains indistinguishable from the initial work—a blank film collecting traces in the process of projection—can we still ascribe authorship to Paik? Perhaps, in this case, the artist's intention would remain the sanctioning authority. Or rather, because of the evident difference between a linear or looped projection and a fragment of clear film later distributed in a plastic box, should the Fluxus edition of *Zen for Film* be assigned a Paik-Maciunas co-authorship? Frankly, hasn't it gone beyond Paik's initial concept and become a separate piece altogether?

—

Zen for Film as contained in *Fluxfilm Anthology* offers us yet another conundrum. An analogue version of *Fluxfilm Anthology* will collect physical marks and traces on Paik's blank film leader over time. A digital version, however—with its finite relation to time, fixation, and subversion of the film's conceptual logic—lacks the aspect of having collected traces other than those produced digitally. Just like a number of films for the programs Maciunas assembled, the initial, analogue variant of *Zen for Film* in the anthology may have been filmed by Moore. *Zen for Film* in the anthology might be regarded as a sort of documentation of one of the film's projections and is thus, like other Fluxfilms from *Fluxfilm Anthology*, highly valuable as historic evidence. Because the film has been screened on various occasions (for example, at Tate Liverpool) and is also available digitally on YouTube (regardless of its legal status), the author and the cinematographer of the *Fluxfilm Anthology* version are equally essential not only for the construction of the identity of Paik's film but also in mediating what it is, including the aspect of distributed authorship that both the anthology and its films inherit.

Compiling editions and multiples, designing posters, flyers, and labels in accordance with Fluxus's collective endeavor, Maciunas suggested a complex and hybrid authorial model. So, for instance, a number of Fluxfilms, such as *Eyeblink* (Yoko Ono), *Dance* (Dick Higgins), and *10 Feet* (Maciunas) were initially uncredited. Although Maciunas does credit Moore as the filmmaker, the performers in some of these Fluxfilms remain anonymous.[10] Maciunas saw Fluxus as "a collective never promoting prima donnas at the expense of other members."[11] Even when only an individual piece was performed at concerts and festivals, he insisted on crediting the entire Fluxus collective so as to benefit all Fluxus members. Maciunas promoted "collective spirit, anonymity and ANTI-INDIVIDUALISM."[12] He believed that "eventually we would destroy the authorship of pieces and make them totally anonymous—thus eliminating artists' 'ego'—[the] author would be 'Fluxus.'"[13]

—

Following the cyclical logic of reinstallation or reperformance, the presence of instructions or a score and an artwork's allographic quality sanction continuity but also complicate questions of authorship. Fluxus event scores blur the boundaries between the performer and the composer far more decisively than musical scores.[14] For instance, Paik's performance (mentioned in revision 2) of *Composition 1960 #10* by La Monte Young ("draw a straight line and follow it") became Paik's *Zen for Head*, presented during the Fluxus Internationale Festspiele Neuester Musik in Wiesbaden in 1962. Young appeared surprised by Paik's coopting authorship of the work and claimed: "I always understood it was my piece."[15] The generally open status of works of art in Fluxus created a practice of answering one composition with another. In this context, the creation of films that entirely eliminate the image so as to foreground the filmic process (for example, John Cavanaugh's flickering *Fluxfilm no. 5*, 1965) might equally be seen as a direct response to Paik's *Zen for Film*.

—

Fluxus's open status and its relation to questions of authorship recalls Umberto Eco's *The Open Work* (originally published in Italian in 1962, during the early days of the Fluxus movement). Attempting to account for the apparently divergent characteristics of modern and traditional art, *The Open Work* draws on an analysis of contemporaneous instrumental music (Stockhausen, Luciano Berio, Henri Pousseur, and Pierre Boulez) in a consideration of the subjective element in interpretation and the role of interpreters in completing a work of art. Discussing Stockhausen's *Klavierstück XI* (1952), Eco observes the increasing autonomy granted to the performer with regard to how a work is played, so that the interpretation of a work becomes an improvisation based on the performer's own discretion.[16] As opposed to Arnold Schoenberg, who, at least at a certain point in his career, attempted to limit the performer's role in the execution of a musical work,[17] composers of open works "reject the definitive, concluded message and multiply the formal possibilities of the distribution of their elements."[18] These works appeal to the initiative of a performer and hence are incomplete and infinite. The author of such an "unfinished" work passes it on to the performer in the form of a "construction kit."[19] The instructions may prescribe specific repetition along defined coordinates, but they allow a performer to interpret them aesthetically and complete the work. Thus, the openness of the artwork in Eco's sense manifests itself already at the social level of execution and collaboration but is not exhausted by it.

—

Another aspect of Eco's consideration of the openness of the artwork concerns its relation to the listener or viewer. *The Open Work* acknowledges the personal perspective of the individual "addressee" of a work of art, whose responses are shaped by his or her own cultural background, tastes, inclinations, and prejudices. Although Eco does not explore the specific nature of the addressee's creative involvement,[20] the artwork, he claims, may only be aesthetically validated from the perspective of the subjective views of its addressees. "It is the viewers who make the pictures," posits Duchamp. Arguing against traditional literary criticism, literary theorist Roland Barthes proclaims the death of the author and the birth of the reader,[21] while Michel Foucault argues in turn that in modern writing, "the mark of the writers is reduced to nothing more than the singularity of his absence."[22] For Foucault the "author" is a function of the written work itself, part of its structure; the historical author must be removed from the interpretive process. Of even greater relevance for *Zen for Film* is Dutton's focus on the audience, which brings a "living critical tradition" to a performance.[23] Taking opera performances at Milan's *La Scala* as an example, Dutton suggests that the particular character of the audience (and its connoisseurship) renders the spectacle complete.[24] If that were the case, would the beholders of and participants in *Zen for Film*'s spectacle be coauthors of the work?

Setting aside this intriguing proposition, I would like to reflect on the curatorial and conservation role in shaping *Zen for Film*'s identity. As the philosopher and art critic Boris Groys asserts, traditionally, the social function of the exhibition was fixed: the artist authored the work, while the curator selected and exhibited it.[25] According to Groys, art is defined by an identity between selection and creation: "the author is someone who selects, who authorizes."[26] In this he follows Duchamp, who turned the act of selection into an act of creation. For Groys, the author is also a curator; thus, installations might be seen as exhibitions curated by artists, sometimes involving ready-mades or objects selected from life (such as, perhaps, the film leader and projector in *Zen for Film*).[27] Because curators select not only artworks by artists but also objects of everyday life, the distinction between artists and curators becomes, for Groys, obsolete.[28] His argument is unlikely to be accepted within the tradition-driven model of artist-genius. If he were persuasive, an artwork would be defined simply as an exhibited object, created by multiple authors.

Regardless of whether we agree with Groys, I suggest that a changeable artwork—one that exists only while displayed, depending on a social rather than an individual effort for its actualization—can be likened to the aspects of distributed authorship that are inherent in all collaborative works.[29] Such actualization requires an archive that includes instructions (either in the form of a physical script or as implicit knowledge) as well as the memory, tacit knowledge, and skill of those involved.[30] The archive as a source of materiality, harboring the identity of an artwork, is oriented both toward the present and toward the past.[31] The limits of the changeability of artworks depend on both archival permissions and the judgments of those involved in making decisions, which are subject to ruling conventions and cultures that determine the contours of what can be said or made.

In addition to the roles that artists' collaborators, technicians, and assistants play in distributed authorship, conservators and curators take on a new role as well, becoming creative agents. Of course, we can question whether a curator's or conservator's creative agency is of the same kind as an artist's. But can a work executed entirely by an assistant, presented by a curator, and modified by a conservator still be ascribed to a single author? Examples of such artworks, created within the framework of post-studio or post-conceptual practice, can no doubt be found outside of Paik's oeuvre.

Although curation claims to be guided by fidelity to the historical record and artistic intention, it appears to enjoy increasing interpretive freedom in relation to successive actualizations of *Zen for Film* in various exhibitions. In contrast, steering clear of the creative process for decades in accordance with its codified professional ethics,[32] traditional conservation still remains trapped in the convention of fidelity to "authentic" material. Yet as philosopher and art historian Hans Ulrich Reck asserts, "conservation is not a later born servant but the present co-author of an authentic work."[33] Reck's admittedly ambitious claim resonates with Groys's earlier assertion that curatorial activities should be regarded as creative acts.[34] Accordingly, the museum, rather than safeguarding the "authentic object," would co-create the identity of the work through conservation and curatorial practice. A more comprehensive view of an artwork may be necessary, one that acknowledges various moments in the artwork's trajectory that are marked by the authorship of the initial idea, the authorship of amendments and modifications, and the authorship of curatorial display. But would such a view ask us to accept uncritically the creative handling of a work by diverse stakeholders, the fabrication, for instance, of *Zen for Film*'s variants, as well as a radical limitation of its display?

Let us conclude this consideration of distributed authorship with *Fluxus Codex* itself. Jon Hendricks's assemblage involves an authorial character similar to that of a curator's assemblage of objects within a defined space. In a certain sense, Hendricks's *Fluxus Codex*, including *Addenda I* and *Addenda II*, exercises authority over the archival ordering, naming, classifying, and reordering of information. Hendricks's effort to establish archival order has the effect of codifying Fluxus, which does not, however, diminish the immense value of *Fluxus Codex* as a resource.

Notes

1—Scholarship on the social aspect of artistic (and artisanal) practice in the workshops of medieval and Dutch painters has challenged the traditional view. For a discussion of studio, intentionality, and individual genius, see Jones, *Machine in the Studio.*

2—The concept of authorship has been explored, for instance, in Richter, "Fluxus;" Higgins, "Enversioning Fluxus."

3—See Becker, *Art Worlds.*

4—See *Addenda I,* 4. Maciunas himself often contributed to the editions, incorporating his own objects.

5—Ibid.

6—The Fluxus edition viewable on the website of the Walker Art Center is labeled differently from the one in the Andersch collection, housed in the archives of the Nam June Paik Art Center in Seoul.

7—See *Addenda I*, 177–78. Both Flux-Kits are from the Silverman Fluxus collection.

8—*Fluxus Codex*, 27.

9—Ibid., 65. Vautier responded to this proposition by stating that he never made loops but rather films.

10—See Ganz, "An Introduction to the Fluxfilm," 3.

11—*Addenda I,* 159.

12—Maciunas, January 1964, quoted in Hendricks, *Fluxus Codex*, 37.

13—*Addenda II,* 167.

14—See Kotz, "Post-Cagean Aesthetics and the 'Event' Score," 81.

15—Neuburger, "Terrific Exhibit," 37. The Fluxus scholar Simon Anderson contends that Paik's *Zen for Head* was one of a series of performances of Young's score by other artists. Anderson, in discussion with the author, May 2012.

16—Eco, *The Open Work,* 1.

17—In the same vein, Igor Stravinsky, too, emphasized the autonomy of musical work, reducing the performer's role merely to a noninterpretive execution. See Cook, "Between Process and Product."

18—Eco, *The Open Work,* 3.

19—Ibid., 4.

20—See Almenberg, *Notes on Participatory Art*, 95.

21—Barthes, "The Death of the Author," 142–48.

22—Foucault, "What Is an Author?," 143.

23—Dutton, "Authenticity in Art," 269.

24—He heightens the importance of his statement by thinking about an audience made up entirely of tourists. Ibid., 269.

25—Groys, "Multiple Authorship," 92.

26—Ibid.

27—Ibid., 93.

28—Ibid. Groys's argument complicates the question of the point of closure or finalization of an open artwork.

29—The notion of an artwork as a social process establishes another intriguing link with new developments in musicology and the understanding of a musical work including its performance as an irreducibly social phenomenon. For the social component of musical performance, see Cook, "Between Process and Product." For the idea of the artwork as social process, see Altshuler, *Collecting the New*; Graham and Cook, *Rethinking Curating.*

30—For the aspects of memory, tacit knowledge, and skill as a part of the archive and its application to multimedia and changeable artworks, see Hölling, "*Re*:Paik," 242–45.

31—For the concept of the archive as a source of artworks' identity, see ibid., 253–56.

32—The prohibition of the creative involvement of a conservator in the artwork was based on, among others, Cesare Brandi's restoration theory. See Brandi, *Theory of Restoration*, 62.

33—Reck, "Authenticity in Fine Art," 98.

34—Groys, "Multiple Authorship," 96.

10th Revision—

Event, Performance, Process

You can win the game by changing the rules of the game.
—Nam June Paik

In the preceding revisions, I have analyzed *Zen for Film* from the perspective of notions of traditional and conceptual art, theories of musical performance, and concepts of authenticity and authorship. This closing revision considers *Zen for Film* in relation to duration, continuity, and change. Before I delve into this topic,

I must first touch on some assumptions that have come to dominate art and conservation theory, particularly in relation to the concept of the object.

For a considerable time, both art and conservation theories were oriented toward the unchanging, unique, and authentic object. In restoration, the traditional branch of conservation, artworks were regarded as unique things, often characterized by or defined in a single medium, embodying an intention. Because the goal of traditional conservation was to render "objects" stable, change was a negative force, to be arrested and concealed. This view of change also had an impact on the notion of time. As in William Hogarth's allegorical print *Time Smoking a Picture* (ca. 1761), time was associated with the negative aspects of change, such as the yellowing, cracking, and fading of painted layers. With the introduction of changeable artworks in the mid-twentieth century, conservation theories gradually began to shift. New thinking in the field distinguished between the enduring and the ephemeral, which were to be conceptualized and treated as two different conditions of art.

Theoretical discourse had also revolved around the static art object.[1] Since the late 1950s, however, artworks gradually became associated with action, performance, happenings, and events. "'Art' is an artwork not as long as it endures, but when it happens," claimed German art theorist and psychologist Friedrich Wolfram Heubach.[2] In a similar vein, American critic Harold Rosenberg turned from the artifactual "thingness" to the act of painting itself. The painting, as an event, results in the physical evidence of a completed set of actions.[3] Responding to Rosenberg, Allan Kaprow imagined painting not as an object but as "an arena of activity and performance."[4] Thus, painting would "shed its status as a gerund and, therefore, regain its status as a verb: a thing happening 'now.'"[5] In other words, an artwork "worked." Fluxus also radically questioned the status of the "art object" both as representation and as a static entity.[6] Art, since Fluxus, was a do-it-yourself enterprise—not, however, a do-it-yourself object, but a do-it-yourself reality. The artists associated with Fluxus rejected the functional, sacrosanct art object, the art object as a commodity and as a vehicle of its own history (although this did not prevent Fluxus from commodifying performances later on).[7] Instead, art became something that happens and transforms; an artwork exists in a state of permanent impermanence.

Thinking about artworks can never be divorced from materiality and endurance. As a conservator, I cannot help but wonder what it means that something, an artwork, is impermanent. Or, with reference to conservation, why does it have to be rendered permanent? Where does the division between the permanent and impermanent come from, and how can we conceive of artworks in relation to this dichotomy? The dichotomy probably arises from the problem of understanding artworks as being in time, as having duration, and has something to do with understanding time in terms of endurance within a human dimension (in other words, understanding permanence measured on a human timescale). Likewise, this problem may connect with the impact on conservation and museum practice of a conservator's or curator's lifespan, which is too short to grasp the temporal passing of a masterpiece. The masterpiece is therefore conceived and must be conserved to endure forever—or at least for the "ever" of a human temporal dimension. This is precisely, I would like to argue, what elicits the idea of a stable, "conservable" object and determines the theories of conservation that I have discussed.

A consideration of the temporal aspect of artworks evokes Gotthold Ephraim Lessing's division between spatial and temporal art[8] and the critique of that division in media and art theories.[9] Spatial art has qualities similar to temporal art but might be viewed as "slow" rather than "fast."[10] This temporal definition allows us to identify a medium's active and passive response to time and to differentiate among the ways various media undergo change. Artworks such as media installations, performances, and events that actively engage time experience faster change; "slower" artworks, such as painting and sculpture, respond passively to time, which becomes reflected in the aging, degradation, and decay of their physical materials. In its cinematic manifestation, *Zen for Film*'s constant readiness to shed its physical freight makes it an artwork that actively responds to time. On the artifactual level, the Fluxus editions and relics accept the passage of time, clearly visible in the brittle celluloid and the yellowed labels and plastic casings.

With this in mind, rather than thinking about permanence versus impermanence, let us reconsider artworks in terms of their relative duration, as British performance artist Stuart Brisley suggests: "The issue is not one of the ephemeral versus the permanent. Nothing is forever. It is the question of the relative durations of the impermanent."[11] Accordingly, one could focus attention not on the problematic permanent/impermanent dichotomy but on the aesthetics and qualities of change, accepting change as a positive value with regard to works of both short and long duration.

Artworks such as events, performances, and processes often require textual stabilization: scores, instructions, scripts, testimonies, and digital narratives; they also generate a vast number of objects and side products that act against their temporal passing. Documentation (film, video, photography, text), props, costumes and leftovers, requisites and relics all fill in for the absence of the event, ensuring that something tangible, legible, and visible remains. The aesthetics of change might be replaced by the aesthetics of disappearance, in which materials are produced and amassed while the work "disappears." The work's transience generates the urge to preserve and collect, which, in turn, expands the accumulating archive. As in Sigmund Freud's theory of the fetish, this desire to collect physical objects is never stilled. In the context of performance theory, writer and curator Christopher Bedford names this phenomenon "the viral ontology of performance" and relates it to the "long, variegated trace history that begins with the performance, but whose manifestations may extend, theoretically, to infinity" and to the reanimation of performance in a variety of media.[12] In the absence of the event, artworks generate a complex structure of multilayered documentation. Just as the essence of film resides in film stills for Barthes,[13] for art theorist Sven Lütticken the essence of true live performance is in photos, films, video, and descriptions.[14] Whether the existence of such an essence in film and performance can be claimed, focusing attention on their extended residual history is highly relevant for understanding the nature of their sources.

In a sort of genealogical interdependence—in which facsimiles of documents built on other documents, which in turn were built on other documents, become artworks themselves[15]—such "stratigraphy" of documentation may never cease to expand, continually depositing new layers on the already accumulated sediment. New interpretations, technologies, cultures of actualization (permitting certain things while restricting others), and multiple locations in which the work exists or is reinterpreted render the achievement of the totality of an artwork's archive an illusion. Subsequent interpretations will thus rely on fragmented information and will never be unbiased or complete.

From a temporal perspective, *Zen for Film* might thus be conceived of as a performance of sorts, in which the action is enacted by the projector and witnessed by the audience. The mechanical embodiment consists of an apparatus that projects a blank film on a vertical surface. What remains of this performance is a film loop endowed with traces, a temporal marker and reference to the many hours of labor, an individual object to be appreciated for its evidentiary quality. Dependent on the status of the projection and contingent on value judgments regarding what might be permitted to enter the archive (whether the object is deemed valuable, historical, or worthless), the residue of this performance—the used film—is "conservable" and might be preserved. Potentially, it might—just like the earliest film and the boxed Fluxfilm editions—become a signifier of times long past, a fossilized filmic artifact/relic cherished for its link to the past but also precisely for this reason condemned never to see the light of the projector again.

Could this be the motivation behind the museum's desire that filmstrips used during the course of any reinstallation be destroyed? One may speculate that too many leftovers would diminish the value of the relic owned by the museum. The value of the relic rests not only in the singularity of a historical event but also in the commodity value that it acquires over time as a nonreplicable, unique, and fetishized collectable. Such practice may then limit the realization of *Zen for Film* as Paik conceived it, as an infinitely repeatable event. Rather than being final products, according to Dick Higgins's theory of the "exemplativist" nature of artwork, the objects resulting from the realization of such a concept (but also from a notation or a model) are only examples.[16] The practice of imposing limitations on *Zen for Film*'s open character (which pertains not only to the openness of the initial concept but also to Fluxus's open-ended, mass-produced editions) might be understood as an intervention in the symbolic economy of artworks. This practice fosters a consumption of commodified products and is deprived of the open, active, and social process involved in the contingencies and instabilities of *Zen for Film*'s performance.[17]

"Love objects, respect objects," pleads American artist Claes Oldenburg, referring to the creative act of selecting and caring for what remains after a performance.[18] He continues: "Residual objects are created in the course of making the performance and during repeated performances. The performance is the main thing, but when it's over there are a number of subordinate pieces, which might be isolated, souvenirs, or residual objects."[19] These "acted" or "domesticated" objects bear memory and a history that might unfold in the future.[20] They also fulfill the desire to stabilize and preserve objects in accordance with traditional (Western) museological standards. If works are not meant to function as collectable objects but become such (as has *Zen for Film*'s filmic relic), the process of commodification dictated by market economies reinforces conservation and "conservationist" gestures as exemplified in "keeping" the material of the artwork rather than continuing its concept, tradition, or ritual of making. The process of musealization[21] counters disappearance. The wish to cure grief and nostalgia with an object, a fetish, is deeply rooted.

Thinking about the temporal relativity of artworks can have fascinating consequences. If one inverts the standard assumption that an artwork is an object, a question arises as to whether all artworks might be conceived of as temporal entities—either long or short events, performances, or processes. Accordingly, traditional paintings or sculptures would become artworks of long duration. This might also invert conventional thinking in conservation and in curatorial and museum practice. Not only would the ephemeral/permanent dichotomy be revoked but also the problem of grappling with the nature of the "new" (multimedia, performance, event) through the lens of deeply rooted ideas about the old, "stable" object. Indeed, as one more consequence of inverting standard assumptions, traditional artworks could now be approached through the lens of the "new." Seen from a conservation perspective, this inversion seems to be a novelty that requires some attention, although I cannot pursue it here.

Performances or events have a compressed temporal presence but are no less material. Further, the amount of material produced by an artwork might be seen as inversely proportional to its endurance in time. In the process of musealization and commodification—and in response to the urge to secure tangible things, leftovers, props, relics, video, and film—documentation may even acquire the status of the artwork itself.[22] These things, of course, might be kept "forever," satisfying the traditional materialist attitude. This is not to say that long-duration artworks fail to produce documentation—quite the contrary. Nevertheless, the documentation of long-duration works cannot match the mass of documentation and residual objects produced by performance. Compared to long-duration objects, short-duration works are more varied and rich in genre and quantity and in their potential to become artworks. But what would be an analogue of the performance's relics and leftovers for traditional objects? Perhaps the "stable object" is its own relic and remnant, accumulating the strata of its own making and all past interventions (cleaning, retouching, etc.). Although works by acclaimed artists would have the status of a relic, the unsigned painting bought at a thrift shop for five dollars might be conceived of as the leftover of an unappreciated performance.

—

Conceiving of *Zen for Film* as performance recalls the aesthetic theories of philosopher David Davies.[23] His "type" theory stems from Charles Sanders Peirce's semantic distinctions between the words "type" and "token."[24] Generally speaking, this much-debated distinction applies to multiple arts, such as music and photography, and characterizes tokens as examples of a universal type (performances of a musical work, prints of a photograph). Building on Gregory Currie's suspension of the distinction between singular and multiple arts (of which Goodman's theory of symbols is an example), Davies offers a twist on Currie's theory by claiming that all artworks are token events rather than type events.[25] Coinciding with the temporal turn in the arts of the 1960s and its theoretical underpinnings (discussed at the beginning of this revision), Davies's model views the real work as the process, the series of actions by which the artist arrives at his or her product—not the product itself. According to Davies, the painted canvas is a "focus of appreciation" through which we regard the artist's achievement and which embodies the artist's idea and work. The kind of focus determines the physical object; some foci require the analysis of the enactment.[26]

Although it is interesting to identify an artwork in terms of the sort of creative action an artist has undertaken, this approach, if viewed from a reverse perspective, might be pushed further. If one pays careful attention to the modes of an artwork's creation, to how it came into being, the conditions identifying artworks might equally be provided by observing their "afterlives." An artwork's afterlife concerns the time after the work "happened" (in Heubach's sense). This afterlife is important in identifying what and how the artwork is, which is, in fact, the only reality to which we have access. The process of creation does not provide the sole source of information about what an artwork is. Thus, instead of identifying—or rather imagining—the past retroactively, the proposed approach insists on looking at the present. Other options include reenactment, expanded trace history, actualization, and also attention to transition—decay, disintegration, and degradation.

My proposal falls within the realm of "type" theory, but unlike the theory of art as performance, it focuses on what is left—the object, leftovers, props, residues, documentation, and so on.[27] Thus, although both theories concern the question of *when* the artwork is, my approach focuses on a mode of studying artworks that shifts from how and when art was created, to what is left from the creative act, what has become of it in the present—the only reality and point of access to the work. Consequently, the shift from product art (traditional artworks) to process art (artworks after the temporal turn among artists in the 1960s and in art critical theory) entails a concern with that which *remains*.[28] It follows then that artworks might be identified in relation to their temporal characteristics, so that they are understood as durational, yet distinct. In performance, the defining parameters are duration and intensity.[29] Although subject to the relativity of judgment, these qualities make it possible to distinguish, depending on context, among event, performance, process, and object and to overcome the opposition between the permanent and the impermanent artwork. In fact, *Zen for Film* presents us with an entire range of temporal durations. Although, as I have stressed, the distinctions among the categories of event, performance, process, and object are relative, if Paik's film is conceptualized within a particular context, it might be grasped as an event (a nonrepeatable cinematic event), a performance (a performed spectacle, dependent on the length of the viewer's engagement), a process (accumulating traces while it is projected), and an object (an apparatus, filmic props, Fluxfilms, and filmic remnant/relic).

The strategies of event-based artworks such as *Zen for Film* reflect the ways in which the works are conceived. Countering the historical ban on reproduction,[30] performance may be reenacted, process redone. Despite the singularity and irreducibility of the experiential qualities of an event, one must recognize that the event will be repeated, even if differently.[31] According to Deleuze, recurring iterations always involve deferral and difference.[32] And yet the "technique" of repetition does not apply to artworks as physical objects. Because it is not compliant with prevailing museological and conservation culture, such a redoing of an object will always be classified as a copy or, in more derogatory terms, a forgery, depending on valency, rules, and legislation. And yet, do performance, event, and process not result in "objects/originals"?

The notion of forgery recalls Goodman's distinction between forgeable/autographic and unforgeable/allographic art. Generally, allographic art may be characterized by short duration; autographic, by long duration. To stress the temporal dimension of my argument and draw attention to another of its aspects, I would like to replace allographicity and autographicity with Michael Century's neologisms "allochronicity" and "autochronicity." Century employs these terms in relation to the specificity of scores.[33] To apply Century's terms to the temporal relativity of artworks, "allochronic" would refer to artworks that are not tethered to a specific temporality and that are reperformable, while "autochronic" would designate artworks that have a specific, fixed relation to time. Autochronic artworks are those previously treated as long-duration, quasi-stable objects; allochronic artworks may reoccur in repeated iterations.

Zen for Film's relic would thus assume the character of an autochronic entity, while *Zen for Film* projections would be allochronic. Again, this distinction is only viable in the context of traditional Western museological (and conservation) culture, in which the replication of the long-duration artwork is not accepted as a valid strategy for its continuation. Staying close in its relationship to "token" theory by denying the division between multiple and singular artworks, the concepts of autochronicity and allochronicity assure an artwork's location in a time structure and its identity as a temporal entity.

—

In sum, the turn taken by artworks created in the post-Cagean era, such as *Zen for Film*, not only reflects a general change in the concept of art, of what art can be, but also elicits a shift in thinking about its presentation and continuity. If we consider the order of things in conservation and curation seriously, apart from its theoretical implications, the suspension of the distinction between traditional "enduring" objects and "ephemeral" short-duration objects would release us from the antinomies of everyday museological practice. Instead of asking conservators to perform the impossible feat of arresting change, we could think of artworks of all kinds as ever-changing and evolving entities that continually undergo physical alterations and transitions. Accordingly, curation and conservation might be grasped as temporal interventions in artworks. Rather than assigning regenerative capabilities to conservation (through which the artwork is sometimes wondrously returned to its "original state"), the conservator would instigate just another change in the work in its long- or short-duration existence, compliant with archival and cultural permissions and/or limitations. As I have suggested, an artwork's own archive, dependent on the cultures of conservation, establishes rules and sets limits on what can be said or made, with reference to the present as well as the past.

Although performance theories may not be the only way to continue this inquiry, I believe that they offer an opportunity to rethink traditional objects in terms of duration. This, in turn, can expose the hidden deficiencies of long-applied theories and free us once and for all from a blind faith in the permanence of objects that has for too long prevented us from understanding the inherent reality of change.

Notes

1—See Merewether and Potts, introduction to *After the Event*, 5.

2—"'Kunst' ist ein Kunstwerk nicht so lange, wie es hält, sondern passiert." Heubach, "Zur Happening und Fluxus," n.p. (author's translation).

3—Rosenberg, "The American Action Painters."

4—See Kaprow, "The Legacy of Jackson Pollock," 1–9.

5—See McClure, "Notes on Adhesion," 14.

6—Some scholars set themselves against the view that the object of study in art history is the "art object." For instance, Whitney Davis, speaking against the idea of wholeness, completeness, or the self-sufficiency of artworks, claims that "there is no such thing" as an "art object." He continues: "If there is such a thing, it should interest physicists and not art historians." Davis, *Replications*, 2.

7—The minimalist art object (or "object-art") becomes theatrical for Michael Fried, who associates minimalism with a certain form of performativity. Fried, "Art and Objecthood."

8—Lessing, "Laocoön."

9—For instance, McLuhan questioned Lessing's distinction as soon as he became aware of Einsteinian physics. His concept of writing as a spatialization of speech complicates Lessing's notion of the temporal aspect of poetry. See Cavell, *McLuhan in Space*, 118.

10—See my argument in Hölling, "*Re*:Paik," 188–90.

11—Brisley, "The Photographer and the Performer," 83.

12—Bedford, "The Viral Ontology of Performance," 78.

13—See Barthes, "The Third Meaning," 41–62.

14—See Lütticken, "An Arena in Which to Reenact," 24.

15—Mike Kelley's *The Parasite Lilly* (1980) displayed on the occasion of *The Rituals of the Rented Island* (Whitney Museum of American Art, October 31, 2013–February 2, 2014) might serve as an example. Rehearsal documentation, film, photographs, facsimiles, slides, and digital reproduction were only some elements of its complex stratigraphy of documentation.

16—Higgins, "An Exemplativist Manifesto," in *A Dialectic of Centuries*, 156. For a discussion of Higgins's manifesto, see Balsom, "Original Copies," 104.

17—My argument approximates a similar debate in musicology concerning the grasp of a musical work in terms of performance rather than as a product-commodity. For a related discussion, see Cook, "Between Process and Product." For contingencies and instabilities of the event and their relation to performance as a primary postmodern mode, see Nick Kaye, *Postmodernism and Performance*.

18—Oldenburg, "Residual Objects."

19—Ibid.

20—See Brignone, "So Specific Objects," 67.

21—"Musealization" is a concept introduced by the Czech museologist Zbynek Stransky for the adaptation of an artwork from its primary context to a museological context. My use of "musealization" refers primarily to the adaptation of a work of art to the demands and policies of the institution harboring it.

22—Paul Thek, who desperately sought support to keep the residues of his process-oriented installations, is an example, as is Joseph Beuys, who practiced "religious conservation" of his artworks. For a discussion of the iconization of Beuys's performance artifacts, see Mignon and Bourgelles, *Not to Play with Dead Things*, 19.

23—Davies, *Art as Performance*.

24—Peirce, "Prolegomena to an Apology for Pragmaticism."

25—For a discussion of Currie's suspension of the distinction between type and token, see Davies, *Art as Performance*, 127–45. For Goodman's theory of symbols, see Goodman, *Languages of Art*. For Davies's twist on Currie's theory, see Davies, *Art as Performance*, 146–76. For a general discussion of these theories, see Rohrbaugh, "Ontology of Art."

26—For an artwork as a "performance that specifies a focus of appreciation," see Davies, *Art as Performance*, 146–76 (quote on p. 146).

27—For an intriguing perspective on art as documentation, see Groys, "Art in the Age of Biopolitics," 53–66.

28—Further, because no artwork exists outside the context of that which remains of it, the medium (in both its material and immaterial form) might become identifiable through the change it experiences. It is the transition, deterioration, remediation, emulation, and reenactment that offer a point of access to the understanding of the nature of changeable works.

29—In this context, it seems more fruitful to think about time in terms of intensity than in terms of spatialized, mechanized time measurement.

30—See Phelan, *Unmarked*, 3.

31—For the possibility of repetition of an event, see Heathfield, "Then Again," 31.

32—Deleuze maintains that if there were no difference in repetition, things would be identical: repetition is opposed to the fixity and identity of representation. Deleuze, *Difference and Repetition*.

33—Musical theorist and composer Century contrasts the open, improvisational, and allochronic character of the score on a continuum with the closed, routine, autochronic score. Michael Century (professor of new media and music, Rensselaer Polytechnic Institute, Troy, NY), in discussion with the author, October 2013.

Installation, cinematic experience, object, performance, or relic—or all of them at once—*Zen for Film* resists simple classification and categorization. One of the most frequently exhibited among Paik's artworks, *Zen for Film* has from its inception developed a complex trajectory that is mirrored by the uneasiness of its existence within the traditional museum system, complicated even further by the tangled rules created for its archiving and presentation. Such complexity is the result of the impossibility of defining what the work is. With the shift in the understanding of art in the post-Cagean era, *Zen for Film* has been liberated from the attachment to material, on the one hand, while it generates physical traces, on the other. As dictated by the division between the instructions and their physical manifestation, *Zen for Film* submits to the cyclical principle of de- and rematerialization and the logic of repetition and reenactment. This redemptive quality opens up a wide terrain for conceptualizing *Zen for Film*'s manifold materiality and visuality.

By the same token, *Zen for Film* fails to satisfy clear chronological and stylistic definitions—perhaps a sign that they have become anachronistic methods of art historical inquiry. Although the work emerged at the time when conceptual, pop, and video art were gaining momentum, it became a product of more than five decades of continuous reinterpretation, resulting in multiple versions, variations, and editions. This unexhausted history stretches back to the moment when, for the very first time, Paik wound his film on the spools of a projector. In the life of *Zen for Film*, all events are equally significant, validating its trajectory as a continuously evolving process, refusing closure.

So, perhaps, rather than considering the genesis of *Zen for Film*, we may turn to its ontogenesis,[1] characterized by the never-exhausted multiplicity of its temporal existence, plural iterations, and generated residues. In these terms, Heubach's assertion of an artwork's temporality might be turned into the question of whether the artwork *is* or still has to *become* (or, in Heubach's sense, "happen") a truly open work, enriched by future scenarios, attitudes, and cultures, bound to, and generative of, an archive. "Today, the only works that really count are those which are no longer works at all," suggests Theodor Adorno.[2] Opposing the paradigmatic stasis of objects in art history and traditional conservation—and articulating the set of processes through which the work is generated, disseminated, and presented—*Zen for Film* critically intervenes in institutional politics and art economies as well as in the process of writing art history. Floating between established genres and classifications, *Zen for Film* questions what makes an object "collectable" by introducing openness and changeability to long-established formulations. It also has a critical impact on the process of transforming the museum's role in stewardship, including curatorial and conservation practice. *Revisions* contributes to this process by pointing out a few connections among genres, media, concepts, and theories, sketching an image of the cultural-technical inspirations, aspirations, and implications of Paik's *Zen for Film* since the 1960s.

Although my narrative strives to expose *Zen for Film*'s changeable existence and behavior, it has by no means exhausted all possible avenues of inquiry into Paik's artwork, nor is it conclusive. A consideration of other contexts—for instance, the aspect of intellectual property in terms of geographically specific legislation—has remained outside the framework of this project. Similarly, I have chosen not to elaborate on the modes of the viewer's participatory engagement with the artwork in the context of both installation art and cinematic event. These topics and others remain to be explored. The implications of my study of a single work could be evaluated in the context of other artworks created in the post-Cagean era that function as iterant materializations, sanctioned by the collections harboring them and shaped by events and actors involved in various stages of their trajectories. I have also emphasized the role of conservation, which, together with curation, acts at the intersection of disciplines as a cultural practice. The kind of thinking in the expanded field of curation and conservation presented throughout this book and exhibition should serve to foster an acknowledgment of change and impermanence—an element inherent to Zen philosophy, with which *Revisions* began. My meditation about, and enabled by, *Zen for Film* leads us to an acceptance of changeability in media as a condition for the possibility of their endurance and survival. In the words of Don DeLillo: "I've got death inside me. It's just a question of whether or not I can outlive it."[3] Or, if we believe Sigmund Freud: "Transience value is scarcity value in time."[4]

Notes

1—Heathfield writes of a performance's "ontogeneses: the many natures of its becomings." Heathfield, "Then Again," 32.

2—Adorno, *The Philosophy of Modern Music*, 30.

3—The character Jack Gladney makes the statement in Don DeLillo's *White Noise* (New York: Penguin, 1984), 150.

4—Sigmund Freud, "On Transience," 305.

Bibliography

Adorno, Theodor. *The Philosophy of Modern Music.* Translated by Anne G. Mitchell and Wesley V. Blomster. London: Sheed and Ward, 1973.

Almenberg, Gustaf. *Notes on Participatory Art: Toward a Manifesto Differentiating It from Open Work, Interactive Art and Relational Art.* Central Milton Keynes, UK: AuthorHouse, 2010.

Altshuler, Bruce, ed. *Collecting the New: Museums and Contemporary Art.* Princeton, NJ: Princeton University Press, 2005.

Anderson, Simon. "Fluxus: Early Years and Close Correspondences." Master's thesis, Royal College of Art, London, 1983.

Austin, J. L. *How to Do Things with Words.* Cambridge, MA: Harvard University Press, 1962.

Baas, Jacquelynn. *Fluxus and the Essential Questions of Life.* Chicago: University of Chicago Press, 2011.

Balsom, Erika. "Original Copies: How Film and Video Became Art Objects." *Cinema Journal* 53, no. 1 (Fall 2013): 97–118.

Barthes, Roland. *Camera Lucida.* 1980. London: Vintage, 2000.

———. "The Death of the Author." In *Image-Music-Text,* edited and translated by Stephen Heath, 142–48. New York: Hill and Wang, 1978.

———. "The Third Meaning: Research Notes on Some Eisenstein Stills." In *Image, Music, Text,* edited and translated by Stephen Heath, 52–68. London: Fontana, 1970.

Bazin, André. "The Ontology of the Photographic Image." In *What Is Cinema?*, edited by Hugh Gray, 9–16. Berkeley: University of California Press, 1967.

Becher, Jürgen, and Wolf Vostell, eds. *Happenings, Fluxus, Pop Art, Nouveau Réalisme.* Hamburg, Germany: Rowohlt, 1965.

Becker, Howard. *Art Worlds.* Berkeley: University of California Press, 2008.

Bedford, Christopher. "The Viral Ontology of Performance." In *Perform, Repeat, Record: Live Art in History,* edited by Amelia Jones and Adrian Heathfield, 77–87. Chicago: Intellect, 2012.

Belting, Hans. "Beyond Iconoclasm: Nam June Paik; The Zen Gaze and the Escape from Representation." In *Iconoclash: Beyond the Image Wars in Science, Religion, and Art,* edited by Bruno Latour and Peter Weibel, 390–411. Cambridge, MA: MIT Press, 2002.

Benjamin, Walter. "The Work of Art in the Age of Its Technological Reproducibility: Second Version." Translated by Edmund Jephcott and Harry Zohn. In *Walter Benjamin: Selected Writings,* vol. 3: *1935–1938,* edited by Howard Eiland and Michael W. Jennings, 101–33. Cambridge, MA: Belknap Press of Harvard University Press, 2002.

Bird, Jon, and Michael Newman. Introduction to *Rewriting Conceptual Art,* edited by Jon Bird and Michael Newman, 1–11. London: Reaktion, 1999.

Block, René. *1962 Wiesbaden Fluxus 1982: Eine kleine Geschichte von Fluxus in drei Teilen.* Wiesbaden, Germany: Harlekin Art, 1983.

Block, René, and Tobias Berger. "What Is Fluxus?" In *What's Fluxus? What's Not! Why / O que é Fluxus? O que não é! O porquê,* edited by Jon Hendricks, 38–43. Rio de Janeiro: Centro Cultural Banco do Brasil; Detroit, Michigan: Gilbert and Lila Silverman Fluxus Collection, 2002.

Blom, Ina. "Boredom and Oblivion." In Friedman, *The Fluxus Reader,* 63–90.

———. "The Intermedia Dynamics: An Aspect of Fluxus." PhD diss., University of Oslo, 1993.

Bois, Yve-Alain, Branden W. Joseph, Rebecca Y. Kim, Liz Kotz, James Pritchett, and Julia Robinson. *The Anarchy of Silence: John Cage and Experimental Art.* Barcelona: Museu d'Art Contemporani de Barcelona, 2010.

Branden, Joseph W. *Random Order: Robert Rauschenberg and the Neo-Avant-Garde.* Cambridge, MA: MIT Press, 2003.

Brandi, Cesare. *Theory of Restoration.* Translated by Cynthia Rockwell. Florence: Nardini, 2005.

Brignone, Patricia. "So Specific Objects." In *Not to Play with Dead Things,* edited by Eric Mangion and Marie de Brugerolle, 61–73. Zurich: JRP | Ringier, 2009.

Brill, Dorothée. *Shock and the Senseless in Dada and Fluxus.* Hanover, NH: UPNE, 2010.

Brisley, Stuart. "The Photographer and the Performer." In *Live Art on Camera,* edited by Alice Maude-Roxby, 83–88. Southampton, UK: John Hansard Gallery, 2008.

Butt, John. *Playing with History: The Historical Approach to Musical Performance.* Cambridge: Cambridge University Press, 2002.

Cage, John. "Indeterminancy." In *Silence: Lectures and Writings*, 98–109. Middletown, CT: Wesleyan University Press, 1973.

———. "On Robert Rauschenberg, Artist, and His Work." In *Silence: Lectures and Writings*, 98–109. Middletown, CT: Wesleyan University Press, 1973.

———. *Silence: Lectures and Writings*. Middletown, CT: Wesleyan University Press, 1973.

———. "Zum Werk von Nam June Paik." In *Nam June Paik: Video Time—Video Space*, edited by Toni Stoss and Thomas Kellein, 21–26. Ostfildern-Ruit, Germany: Cantz, 1991.

Cavell, Richard. *McLuhan in Space: A Cultural Geography*. Toronto: University of Toronto Press, 2002.

Cook, Nicolas. "Between Process and Product: Music and/as Performance." *The Online Journal of the Society for Music Theory* 7, no. 2 (April 2001). Accessed March 21, 2015. http://www.mtosmt.org/issues/mto.01.7.2/mto.01.7.2.cook.html#FN16REF.

Daniels, Dieter. "Vier Fragen an John Cage." *Fluxus—Ein Nachruf zur Lebzeiten, Kunstforum*, no. 115 (1991): 214.

Davies, David. *Art as Performance*. Oxford: Blackwell, 2004.

Davies, Stephen. "Authenticity in Musical Performance." *British Journal of Aesthetics* 27 (1987): 39–50.

———. *Musical Works and Performances: A Philosophical Exploration*. Oxford: Clarendon Press, 2001.

Davis, Whitney. *Replications: Archaeology, Art History, Psychoanalysis*. University Park: Pennsylvania State University Press, 1996.

Decker, Edith. *Paik Video*. Cologne: DuMont, 1988.

Deleuze, Gilles. *Cinema 1: The Movement Image*. 1983. Translated by Hugh Tomlinson and Barbara Habberjam. Minneapolis: University of Minnesota Press, 2012.

———. *Difference and Repetition*. 1968. Translated by Paul Patton. New York: Columbia University Press, 1994.

DeLillo, Don. *White Noise*. 1985. New York: Penguin, 2009.

Derrida, Jacques. *Copy, Archive, Signature: A Conversation on Photography*. Edited and with an introduction by Gerhard Richter. Translated by Jeff Fort. Redwood City, CA: Stanford University Press, 2010.

Dezeuze, Anna. "Play, Ritual and Politics: Transitional Artworks in the 1960s." In *The "Do-It-Yourself" Artwork: Participation form Fluxus to New Media*, edited by Anna Dezeuze, 47–68. Manchester, UK: Manchester University Press, 2010.

Dipert, Randall R. "Towards a Genuine Philosophy of the Performing Arts." *Reason Papers* 13 (1988): 182–200.

Doris, David. "Zen Vaudeville: A Medi(t)ation in the Margins of Fluxus." In Friedman, *The Fluxus Reader*, 91–135.

Dörstel, Wilfred, Rainer Steinberg, and Robert von Zahn. "The Bauermeister Studio: Proto-Fluxus in Cologne 1960–62." In *Fluxus Virus*, edited by Christel Schüppenhauer, 56–67. Cologne: Gallery Schüppenhauer, 1992.

Dutton, Denis. "Authenticity in Art." In *The Oxford Handbook of Aesthetics*, edited by Jerold Levinson, 258–74. New York: Oxford University Press, 2003.

Eamon, Christopher. "An Art of Temporality." In *Film and Video Art*, edited by Stuart Comer, 66–85. London: Tate Publishing, 2009.

Eco, Umberto. *The Open Work*. Translated by Anna Cancogni. Cambridge, MA: Harvard University Press, 1989.

Elkins, James. "On Some Limits of Materiality in Art History." *Das Magazin des Instituts für Theorie* [Zürich] 12 (2008): 25–30.

Ernst, Wolfgang. "Media Archaeology: Method and Machine versus History and Narrative of Media." In *Media Archaeologies: Approaches, Applications, and Implications*, edited by Erkki Huhtamo and Jussi Parikka, 239–55. Berkeley: University of California Press, 2011.

Filliou, Robert. "GOOD-FOR-NOTHING-GOOD-FOR-EVERYTHING (c. 1962)." In *Theories and Documents of Contemporary Art: A Sourcebook of Artists' Writings*, edited by Kristine Stiles and Peter Howard Selz, 854. Berkeley: University of California Press, 2012 (1996).

Flynt, Henry. "Concept Art." In *An Anthology of Chance Operations, Indeterminacy, Improvisation, Concept Art, Anti-Art, Meaningless Work, Natural Disasters, Stories, Diagrams, Music, Dance,*

Constructions, Compositions, Mathematics, Plans of Actions, edited by La Monte Young, n.p. New York: La Monte Young and Jackson Mac Low, 1963.

"Fluxfest: In and around Fluxus." In *A Festival of Fluxfilms, Fluxloops, Fluxslides and Environments* (September 19–October 11, 1992), program brochure. New York: Anthology Film Archives, 1992.

Fluxfilm Anthology. Electronic Arts Intermix, online database. Accessed January 5, 2015. http://eai.org/title.htm?id=11976.

Fontana, Lucio. "Manifesto Blanco (1946)." In *Theories and Documents of Contemporary Art: A Sourcebook of Artists' Writings*, edited by Kristine Stiles and Peter Howard Selz, 47–50. Berkeley: University of California Press, 1996.

Foster, Hal, Rosalind Krauss, Yve-Alain Bois, and Benjamin Buchloh, eds. *Art since 1900: Modernism, Antimodernism, Postmodernism*. New York: Thames and Hudson, 2005.

Foucault, Michel. "Of Other Spaces." *Diacritics* 16 (Spring 1986): 22–27.

———. "What Is an Author?" In *Textual Strategies: Perspectives in Post-Structuralist Criticism*, edited by Josué V. Harari, 141–60. 1969. Ithaca, NY: Cornell University Press, 1979.

Freud, Sigmund. "On Transience." In *The Standard Edition of the Complete Psychological Works of Sigmund Freud*, edited and translated by James Strachey, 14:305–6. London: Hogarth, 1953–74.

Fried, Michael. *Art and Objecthood: Essays and Reviews*. Chicago: University of Chicago Press, 1998.

Friedman, Ken, ed. *The Fluxus Reader*. Chichester, UK: Academy Editions, 1998.

———. "Introduction: A Transformative Vision of Fluxus." In Friedman, *The Fluxus Reader*, viii–x.

Ganz, Jim. "An Introduction to the Fluxfilm: Notes on Films in the Gilbert and Lila Silverman Collection." Master's thesis, Williams College Graduate Program in the History of Art, 1988.

Gidal, Peter, ed. *Structural Film Anthology*. London: British Film Institute, 1978.

Goodman, Nelson. *Languages of Art: An Approach to a Theory of Symbols*. 1968. London: Oxford University Press, 1969.

———. *Of Mind and Other Matters*. Cambridge, MA: Harvard University Press, 1984.

Graham, Beryl, and Sarah Cook, eds. *Rethinking Curating: Art after New Media*. Cambridge, MA: MIT Press, 2010.

Greenberg, Clement. "Towards a Newer Laocoön." In *The Collected Essays and Criticism*, vol. 1: *Perceptions and Judgments 1939–1944*, edited by John O'Brian, 23–37. Chicago: University of Chicago Press, 1986.

Groys, Boris. "Art in the Age of Biopolitics: From Artwork to Documentation." In *Art Power*, 53–66. Cambridge, MA: MIT Press, 2008.

———. "Multiple Authorship." In *Art Power*, 100–107. Cambridge, MA: MIT Press, 2008.

Hanhardt, John. *The Worlds of Nam June Paik*. New York: Solomon R. Guggenheim Foundation, 2000.

Heathfield, Adrian. "Then Again." In *Perform, Repeat, Record: Live Art in History*, edited by Amelia Jones and Adrian Heathfield, 27–35. Chicago: Intellect, 2013.

Heidegger, Martin. *The Fundamental Concepts of Metaphysics: World, Finitude, Solitude*, translated by William McNeill and Nicholas Walker. Bloomington: Indiana University Press, 1995.

Hein, Birgit. "On Structural Studies." In *Structural Film Anthology*, edited by Peter Gidal, 114–15. London: British Film Institute, 1978.

Hendricks, Jon, ed. *Fluxus Codex*. Detroit: Gilbert and Lila Silverman Fluxus Collection in association with H. N. Abrams, New York, 1988.

———, ed. *Fluxus Etc.: The Gilbert and Lila Silverman Fluxus Collection*. Bloomfield Hills, MI: Cranbrook Academy of Art Museum, 1981.

———, ed. *Fluxus Etc. / Addenda I: The Gilbert and Lila Silverman Collection*. New York: Ink and Press, 1983.

———, ed. *Fluxus Etc. / Addenda II: The Gilbert and Lila Silverman Fluxus Collection*. Pasadena: California Institute of Technology and Baxter Art Gallery, 1983.

Herzogenrath, Wulf. *Nam June Paik Fluxus / Video*. Munich: Silke Schreiber, 1983.

———."When the Future Was Now: Wulf Herzogenrath on Nam June Paik," *Tate ETC.*, accessed December 23, 2012, http://www.tate.org.uk/tateetc/issue21/namjunepaik.htm.

Heubach, Friedrich Wolfram. "Zur Happening und Fluxus." A brochure accompanying *Happening und Fluxus: Materialien*, edited by Hanns Sohm (Cologne: Kölnischer Kunstverein, 1970).

Higgins, Dick. *A Dialectic of Centuries: Notes towards a Theory of New Arts.* New York: Printed Editions, 1978.

———. "Fluxus: Theory and Reception." In Friedman, *The Fluxus Reader,* 217–36.

———. "Statement on Intermedia." In *Dé-coll/age,* edited by Wolf Vostell. Frankfurt: Typos; New York: Something Else, 1967. Accessible online at http://www.artpool.hu/Fluxus/Higgins/intermedia2.html.

Higgins, Hannah B. "Enversioning Fluxus: A Venture into Whose Fluxus Where and When." PhD diss., University of Chicago, 1994.

Hoffman, Jens, ed. *Ten Fundamental Questions of Curating.* Milan: Mousse Publishing, Fiorucci Art Trust, 2013.

Hölling, Hanna B. *Paik's Virtual Archive: Time, Change, and Materiality in Media Art.* Berkeley: University of California Press, forthcoming.

———. "*Re*:Paik: On Time, Changeability and Identity in the Conservation of Nam June Paik Multimedia Installations." PhD diss., University of Amsterdam, 2013.

Iles, Chrissie, and Henriette Huldisch. "Keeping Time: On Collecting Film and Video Art in Museums." In *Collecting the New: Museums and Contemporary Art,* edited by Bruce Altshuler, 65–83. Princeton, NJ: Princeton University Press, 2005.

Jenkins, Bruce. "Fluxfilm in Three False Starts." In *Art and the Moving Image: A Critical Reader,* edited by Tanya Leighton, 53–71. London: Tate Publishing / Afterall, 2008.

Jones, Caroline A. *Machine in the Studio: Constructing the Postwar American Artist.* Chicago: University of Chicago Press, 1996.

Joseph, Branden W. *Random Order: Robert Rauschenberg and the Neo-Avant-Garde.* Cambridge, MA: MIT Press, 2003.

Kacunko, Slavko. *Closed Circuit Videoinstallationen: Ein Leitfaden zur Geschichte und Theorie der Medienkunst mit Bausteinen eines Künstlerlexikons auf DVD.* Berlin: Logos, 2004.

Kaprow, Allan. "The Legacy of Jackson Pollock." In *Allan Kaprow: Essays on the Blurring of Art and Life,* edited by Jeff Kelley, 1–9. Berkeley: University of California Press, 2003.

———. "Notes on the Creation of a Total Art." In *Critical Mass: Happenings, Fluxus, Performance, Intermedia, and Rutgers University, 1958–1972,* edited by Geoffrey Hendricks, 5–6. New Brunswick, NJ: Rutgers University Press, 2003.

Kaye, Nick. *Postmodernism and Performance.* London: Macmillan, 1994.

Kellein, Thomas. *The Dream of Fluxus: George Maciunas—An Artist's Biography.* London: Hansjörg Mayer, 2007.

———. *Fluxus.* Basel: Kunsthalle Basel, 1994.

Kim, Eunji. *Nam June Paik: Videokunst in Museen; Globalisierung und lokale Rezeption.* Berlin: Reimer, 2010.

Kinsella, Anna R. "Was Recursion the Key Step in the Evolution of the Human Language Faculty?" In *Recursion and Human Language,* edited by Harry van der Hulst, 179–92. New York: Walter de Gruyter, 2010.

Kivy, Peter. *Authenticities: Philosophical Reflections on Musical Performance.* Ithaca, NY: Cornell University Press, 1995.

Knapstein, Gabrielle. "Fluxus." In *DuMonts Begriffslexikon zur zeitgenössischen Kunst,* edited by Hubertus Butin, 86–90. Cologne: DuMont, 2002.

Kosuth, Joseph."Art after Philosophy." *Studio International* (October 1969): 134–37.

Kotz, Liz. "Post-Cagean Aesthetics and the 'Event' Score." *October* 95 (Winter 2001): 55–89.

Krauss, Rosalind. "The Originality of the Avant-Garde." In *The Originality of the Avant-Garde and Other Modernist Myths,* 151–70. Cambridge, MA: MIT Press, 1985.

———. *A Voyage on the North Sea: Art in the Age of the Post-Medium Condition.* London: Thames and Hudson, 2000.

Kubelka, Peter. "Peter Kubelka: Filmmaker." In *Tacita Dean: Film,* edited by Nicholas Cullinan, 92. London: Tate Publishing, 2011.

Landy, Leigh, and Antje von Graevenitz. "I Make Technology Ridiculous—The Unusual Dialectics of Nam June Paik." In *Avant Garde: Technik,* edited by Leigh Landy, 79–108. Atlanta: Rodopi, 1992.

Lee, Pamela M. *Chronophobia: On Time in the Art of the 1960s.* Cambridge, MA: MIT Press, 2004.

Lessing, Gotthold Ephraim. *Laocoön: An Essay upon the Limits of Painting and Poetry,* translated by E. C. Breasley. London: Longman, Brown, Green and Longmans, 1853.

Lewallen, Constance. "Cage and the Structure of Chance." In *Writings through John Cage's Music and Poetry, + Art,* edited by David W. Bernstein and Christopher Hatch, 234–43. Chicago: University of Chicago Press, 2001.

LeWitt, Sol. "Paragraphs on Conceptual Art." *Artforum* 51, no. 10 (June 1967): 79–83. Reprinted in *Theories and Documents of Contemporary Art: A Sourcebook of Artists' Writings,* edited by Kristine Stiles and Peter Howard Selz, 822–26. Berkeley: University of California Press, 2012 (1996).

Lippard, Lucy R. *Six Years: The Dematerialization of the Art Object from 1966 to 1972.* 1973. Berkeley: University of California Press, 1997.

Lütticken, Sven. "An Arena in Which to Reenact." In *Live, Once More: Forms of Re-Enactment in Contemporary Art,* edited by Sven Lütticken, 17–60. Rotterdam: Witte de With Institute, 2005.

Lutz, Albert, ed. *Mystik: Die Sehnsucht nach dem Absoluten.* Zurich: Scheidegger and Spiess, 2011.

Maciunas, George. "Some Comments on 'Structural Film' by P. Adams Sitney (*Film Culture* no. 47, 1969) by George Maciunas." In *Film Culture Reader,* edited by P. Adams Sitney, 349. 1970. New York: Cooper Square, 2000.

McClure, Michael Jay. "Notes on Adhesion: The Object of Art and the Work of Art after Conceptualism." *Performance Research* 12, no. 4 (2007): 14–23.

Meigh-Andrews, Chris. *A History of Video Art.* New York: Bloomsbury Academic, 2006.

Mekas, Jonas. *Movie Journal: The Rise of the New American Cinema, 1959–1971.* New York: Collier, 1972.

Merewether, Charles, and John Potts. Introduction to *After the Event: New Perspectives on Art History,* edited by Charles Merewether and John Potts, 1–6. Manchester, UK: Manchester University Press, 2010.

Mignon, Eric, and Marie de Bourgelles, eds. *Not to Play with Dead Things.* Zurich: JRP | Ringier, 2009.

Moholy-Nagy, László. *The New Vision: Fundamentals of Bauhaus Design, Painting, Sculpture, and Architecture.* New York: W. W. Norton and Co., 1938.

Mulvey, Laura. *Death 24x a Second: Stillness and the Moving Image.* London: Reaktion, 2006.

Neuburger, Susanne. "Terrific Exhibit: 'Time Art' Alias Music in the Exhibition Genre." In *Nam June Paik: Exposition of Music, Electronic Television, Revisited,* edited by Susanne Neuburger, 31–43. Cologne: Walther König, 2009.

Nyman, Michael. "Nam June Paik, Composer." In *Nam June Paik,* edited by John Hanhardt, 79–90. New York: Whitney Museum of American Art, 1982.

Oldenburg, Claes. "Residual Objects" (1962). In *Claes Oldenburg: An Anthology,* 143. New York: Guggenheim Museum, 1995. Accessible online at http://archive.org/stream/claesold00olde/claesold00olde_djvu.txt.

Osborne, Peter. *Conceptual Art: Themes and Movements.* London: Phaidon, 2002.

———. "The Dreambird of Experience: Utopia, Possibility, Boredom." *Radical Philosophy,* no. 137 (May–June 2006): 36–44.

Paik, Nam June. "Afterlude to the Exposition of Experimental Television." *fluxus cc fiVe ThReE* (June 1964). Reprinted in *Theories and Documents of Contemporary Art: A Sourcebook of Artists' Writings,* edited by Kristine Stiles and Peter Howard Selz, 431–33. Berkeley: University of California Press, 1996.

———. "Artificial Intelligence vs Artificial Metabolism." In *Nam June Paik Fluxus/Video,* edited by Wulf Herzogenrath, 252–53. Bremen: Kunsthalle Bremen, 1999.

———. "Beiblatt zur Einladung, 'Exposition of Music,' Galerie Parnass, Wuppertal, 11.03.1963." In *Happening und Fluxus: Materialien,* edited by Hanns Sohm. Cologne: Kölnischer Kunstverein, 1970.

———. *Du cheval à Christo et autres écrits,* edited by Edith Decker and Irmeline Lebeer. Brussels: Lebeer Hossmann, 1993.

Paik, Nam June, and Justin Hoffman. "Interview in a Station Restaurant: Nam June Paik in Conversation with Justin Hoffmann, Wiesbaden, May 22, 1989." In *Nam June Paik: Exposition of Music, Electronic Television, Revisited,* edited by Susanne Neuburger, 83–88. Cologne: Walther König, 2009.

Peirce, Charles Sanders. "Prolegomena to an Apology for Pragmaticism." *Monist* 16, no. 4 (1906): 492–546.

Phelan, Peggy. *Unmarked: The Politics of Performance.* New York: Routledge, 1993.

Phillpot, Clive. "Fluxus: Magazines, Manifestos, *Multum in Parvo.*" In *Fluxus: Selections from the Gilbert and Lila Silverman Collection,* edited by Clive Phillpot and Jon Hendricks, 9–16. New York: Museum of Modern Art, 1988.

Phillpot, Clive, and Jon Hendricks, eds. *Fluxus: Selections from the Gilbert and Lila Silverman Collection.* New York: Museum of Modern Art, 1988.

Pillow, Kirk. "Did Goodman's Distinction Survive LeWitt?" *Journal of Aesthetics and Art Criticism* 61, no. 4 (2003): 365–80.

Pollard, Clare, and John Stevens, eds. *Zen Mind Zen Brush: Japanese Ink Paintings from the Gitter-Yelen Collection.* Sydney: Art Gallery of New South Wales, 2006.

Reck, Hans Ulrich. "Authenticity in Fine Art to the Present Day." In *Wie haltbar ist Videokunst? How Durable Is Video Art?,* edited by Bärbel Otterbeck and Christian Scheidermann, 81–102. Wolfsburg, Germany: Kunstmuseum Wolfsburg, 1995.

Rhee, Jieun. "Reconstructing the Korean Body: Nam June Paik as Specular Border." *Oriental Art* 48, no. 4 (2002): 47–50.

Richter, Dorothee. "Fluxus: Kunst gleich Leben? Mythen um Autorschaft, Produktion, Geschlecht und Gemeinschaft." PhD diss., University of Bremen, 2011.

Rohrbaugh, Guy. "Ontology of Art." In *The Routledge Companion to Aesthetics,* 2nd ed., edited by Berys Gaut and Dominic McIver Lopes, 241–54. New York: Routledge, 2005.

Rosenberg, Harold. "The American Action Painters." *Art News* 51, no. 8 (December 1952): 22–23, 48–49.

Rugoff, Ralph. *Invisible: Art about the Unseen, 1957–2012.* London: Hayward, 2012.

Ruhé, Harry. *Fluxus: The Most Radical and Experimental Art Movement of the Sixties.* Amsterdam: "A", 1976.

Rush, Michael. *Video Art.* London: Thames and Hudson, 2007.

Saper, Craig. "Fluxus as Laboratory." In Friedman, *The Fluxus Reader,* 136–51.

Schmidt-Burkhardt, Astrit, ed. *Maciunas' Learning Machines: From Art History to Chronology of Fluxus.* Berlin: Gilbert and Lila Silverman Fluxus Collection / Vice Versa, Berlin, 2003.

Schüppenhauer, Christel. *Fluxus Virus.* Cologne: Gallery Schüppenhauer, 1992.

Selz, Peter Howard, and Kristine Stiles. "Gestural Abstraction." In *Theories and Documents of Contemporary Art: A Sourcebook of Artists' Writings,* edited by Kristine Stiles and Peter Howard Selz, 13–23. Berkeley: University of California Press, 1996.

Sitney, P. Adams, "Structural Film." In *Film Culture Reader,* edited by P. Adams Sitney, 326–48. New York: Cooper Square, 2000 (1970). First published in *Film Culture,* no. 47 (Summer 1969).

Smith, Owen. "Developing a Fluxable Forum." In Friedman, *The Fluxus Reader,* 3–21.

Sohm, Hanns, ed. *Happening und Fluxus: Materialien.* Cologne: Kölnischer Kunstverein, 1970.

Sontag, Susan. "The Aesthetics of Silence." In *Styles of Radical Will,* 3–34. New York: Farrar, Straus and Giroux, 1969.

Taruskin, Richard. *Text and Act: Essays on Music and Performance.* New York: Oxford University Press, 1995.

Tomkins, Calvin. *The Bride and the Bachelors: Five Masters of the Avant-Garde.* New York: Penguin, 2003.

Truman, James. "Set Pieces." *The Face,* no. 29 (1982): 36–38.

Uroskie, Andrew. *Between the Black Box and the White Cube: Expanded Cinema and Postwar Art.* Chicago: University of Chicago Press, 2014.

Westgeest, Helen. *Zen in the Fifties: Interaction in Art between East and West.* Zwolle, Netherlands: Waanders Uitgevers, 1996.

Zschocke, Nina. *Der irritierte Blick: Kunstrezeption und Aufmerksamkeit.* Munich: Wilhelm Fink, 2006.

Index

F

G

H

I

J

K

L

M

S

T

V

W

Y

Z